When The Closed Heart Opens

Lessons Learned on the Journey of Life

Claudette P. Crouse

ISBN: 978-1-4834-7934-7 (sc)
ISBN: 978-1-4834-7526-4 (e)

Claudette Crouse
CPC Press

Lulu Publishing Services rev. date: 12/12/2017

This book is dedicated to my granddaughter Julia.
May she be a large chip off the old block.

Acknowledgements

$\mathcal{I}$ AM GRATEFUL TO ALL the people who have touched my life and who, in a sense, are the contributing authors of this book. The imprints they made, negative or positive, have formed the ideas, thoughts, and behaviors that helped me to be who I am.

A special thank you to Joyce Williams, who not only read my draft, but also took the time to edit and make corrections throughout the entire book.

A big thank you to Donna Wilmarth who was the first person to read my book and give me supportive feedback.

I have a deep appreciation for my friends who read my drafts and encouraged me to complete the book, citing it was a story worth telling.

A loving thank you to my Bible Study Sisters, Dividend Sisters, and Link Sisters. The special bonds we share have provided the structure and support that have carried me to this place.

My heart is full with love and appreciation for all the people who have touched my life, especially my girlfriends who have had my back through all the seasons, and allowed me to just step out on faith. They have played a role in helping me achieve my goals: Nancy Altman, Anne Ashmore Hudson, Susan Windham Bannister, Vivian Beard, Regan Benson, JudyAnn Bigby, Renee Bridges, Bridgit Brown, Michele Carr, Sylvia Carr, Gloria Clarke, Carolyn Coverdale, Anne Covington, Priscilla Douglas, Fannie Dunaway, Jane Edmonds, Juarez Farrington,

Carmen Fields, Joyce Fredkin, Leslie George, Lynette Glover, Marion Grayer, Betty Hager, Marian Heard, Carolyn Hebsgaard, Kimmie Jackson, Ermajean Jones, Dora Lewin, Pat Long, MaryJo Meisner, Ardell Otten, Colette Phillips, Joan Reals, Diane Suda, Kathy Taylor, Dorothy Terrell, Liz Walker, Shawnda Walker, Gloria White Hammond, Linda Whitlock, Donna Wilmarth, Joyce Williams, Sabrina Williams, Bennie Wiley and Donna Levy Wray.

Your photographs are part of my story.

Preface

My LIFE HAS BEEN a continuous journey in the pursuit of knowledge, understanding, and transformation— all with the intention of finding security, self-fulfillment, and happiness.

In this pursuit, I have used every means open to me and questioned every experience, encounter, or situation, to ascertain any lesson that I could use to further my objective of having a life that was full, desirable, and complete.

This drive for security and fulfillment came from a childhood that was full of trauma and emotional deprivation, and a familial situation of violence, chaos, and psychological abuse.

I was fortunate to have the ability to problem-solve, and to come up with ideas or actions to improve or change my circumstances at an early age. When I was older, I was able to enhance these skills by using a didactic approach to search for the essence of any particular entity— always asking what, how, and why in my search for evidence to reveal the answers to the question to which I was seeking. What do I need to learn, to change or to do, for me to have a complete, full and happy life.

This quest has led me from the depth of depression to the height of internal joy and has allowed me to use my gifts to my fullest potential and create the life I want.

My purpose in writing this book is to share what I learned on my journey while searching for me to help other women create the quality of life they want and desire. I hope that by using my personal experiences and first-hand knowledge they will be able to harness their own power to change their circumstances and transform their lives and reject any information that serves to undermine women's confidence and independence: women should be nice, strong assertive women are bit***s, follow the rules and you will be successful.

THE KNOWLEDGE AND WISDOM I acquired has opened my heart to the constant rhythm and changes in my life and led me to title this book *When the Closed Heart Opens*. My open heart has allowed me to achieve my goal to live my best life, and evolve into my best self. I wish the same for my readers.

Foreword

YOU CAN EASILY DISCOVER what Claudette Crouse is thinking. She will tell you. Transparency is her trademark whether she's revealing an intense victory, a staggering defeat, or deep and inward pain. She puts it all out there. Transparency is stripping away the mask and revealing your heart. It's letting light into an experience so that healing can happen—so that you can learn and others can learn from you. Transparency is not always easy. It is not always comfortable, but it is necessary for a life well lived.

One of my earliest recollections of Claudette is now almost 40 years old. It was one summer afternoon shortly after I moved to the condominium development where she and Henry lived in Lexington, when she came surging into my apartment and my life, all drama and drive, to commiserate about some challenge she was going through. The fact that we had just met was beside the point. She poured out her heart and Henry's heart despite the fact he was not there and unaware of the exposure. I will never forget the openness of her sharing, the flair of her storytelling and the intensity with which she sought the lesson in her crisis. Claudette always seeks the lesson; "What's wrong here? What's right? What does this mean? What can we learn?" Her willingness to wrestle with her own presumptions, to push and prod others' opinions, to grapple with any public or private premise, leaving no stone unturned until the truth, if not revealed, can at least be alluded to—has always been her greatest strength.

Beneath the "hows", the "whys", and "why nots" is a deep and passionate desire to discern what is important in life, what matters. Over the years, I have begun to see Claudette's constant search for knowledge as a model for my own and for yours as well. We must all be zealous seekers in order to know and trust the God we have created and the God who is, to learn how he shows up, what she means, what we are to let go of and what we are to keep from each precious and fleeting moment we have.

Claudette has been witness to and benefactor of many exciting and valuable lessons. Some have come at great cost. That she has chosen to share her learning, and her life, is a gift that should never be taken lightly or for granted. There are jewels in the following pages, some hidden, some in plain sight, but all bearing the flair, the drama and the drive of a woman who has lived her life deeply and well...my friend Claudette Crouse.

-Reverend Liz Walker

PART ONE

Chapter
One

I ONCE READ THAT OUR earliest memories are a reflection of a deep psychological imprint that left marks which impacted our psyche.

One of my earliest memories is of waking up in the middle of the night to the sound of furniture being overturned and a body hitting the wall in my parents' bedroom. They were fighting, and actually hitting each other, at least that is what I envisioned from the sounds I could hear. From what I could understand of their shouting, they had been at a party earlier in the evening during which my mother thought my father had made a pass at some woman.

"Claude, you are a dog!" I heard her shout. "You try to sleep with every GD woman you meet. I saw you leave the room with that woman!"

"Ella, you are f---ing crazy!" my father shouted back. "I did not leave the room with any woman, I only went out to take a smoke."

I pulled the covers over my head and buried my face in the pillow, but could not muffle the sharp smacking sound of my mother slapping my father's face, or the sickening thud as his retaliatory punch knocked her to the floor.

"Drunken b*tch!" he hollered.

"I'm going to leave you! You're always cheating, or beating on me, and you are a low-down dog and a coward for hitting a woman."

"You hit me first!" came his angry retort. "Why don't you go ahead and leave? I wish you would; my life would be much better without you in it!"

Even as I write these words more than six decades later, the pain and terror I felt that night are still with me, and I weep for that little girl and the pain she endured. Though this is the earliest memory that I have of my parents fighting, I'm sure it was not their first and it certainly was not their last physical confrontation. Hearing your parents fighting in the next room would be disturbing to anyone, but to a small child it was crushing. I grew to dread the sound of raised voices. I would rush into their room crying, and screaming to the top of my voice, "Stop it, stop it," often so terrorized that I couldn't stop crying or shaking, even when my parents did stop. I am not sure how often this occurred, but the impact was devastating and I was in a constant state of anxiety. Being a little kid, I thought if they could *hit* each other, then they might actually *kill* each other. *And who,* I would wonder, *would take care of me then?*

In the mornings after one of my parents' altercations, the mood in our house was always dark and somber, with no one talking. Silence. But there would be evidence of what happened the night before, turned over or broken furniture, or physical injuries to one of my parents. Mostly to my mother.

After a while the emotional toll I suffered from their fighting increased to the point that I became psychology impaired—fearful, anxious, and unable to sleep. The slightest provocation between my parents would cause me to break out into tears. Seeing how emotionally raw I was began to worry them, and they suspended their fighting for a while. But the damage to my psyche was done, and from then on, even when I got older, I was unable to cope when someone was mean or disagreeable towards me. My reaction would be to yell, scream, hang-up the phone or leave, instead of talking and explaining my feelings.

The respite from my parent's fighting didn't last, and in time, they were brawling again. Of course, my mother was no match for my father, so not surprisingly, she usually came out on the losing end—with bruises or a black eye, and in one case a broken shoulder. But this never seemed to deter her from engaging in the battle. The driving force behind their conflict was their jealousy. My father was a very handsome man with finely sculpted features, a smooth jaw, soft eyes, and a presence that seemed to attract women like bees to honey. He was also introverted, aloof, and void of any sense of rhythm. This was probably the root of his jealousy when my mother, who was a great dancer, danced with someone else. My mother was also quite attractive, tall for a woman of her time, with a slim figure. She dressed in beautiful clothes, and usually wore her hair drawn back in a bun.

I can recall a big fight my parents had after my mother won a dance contest with another man. My father accused her of dancing like a slut.

"Claude that is the way the dance goes," I heard her say. "My partner went down to the floor, so I went down to the floor with him. That is why we won the dance contest."

My father said it was too suggestive, and made her look whorish. If memory serves me, I think the dance was named "The Hucklebuck", so-named for the steps in which dancers' bodies bucked like wild steers to the rhythm of the music.

When I heard my parents coming home from a party, I often felt my heart was about to stop. I would pray that my mother would not start an argument that would end up with them fighting. Whenever possible, I would ask my parents to let me stay over with a girlfriend on the weekends so I could avoid their quarrels. The only person I ever told about my home situation was my friend Meg.

My mother was often unkind to me, but this was nothing compared to how Meg's mother treated her and her little sister. Meg's mother, Mrs. Jones, was a drinker, and she always had a house full of friends. Often, she would wake Meg up in the middle of the night to have her demonstrate some new dance for her friends. Mrs. Jones was both verbally and physically abusive to her and her little sister Jeannie. But Jeannie received the brunt of Mrs. Jones' physical abuse, and got frequent beatings. Once, her mother put Jeannie in a tub of scalding water, and the scars were still visible the day I went to visit Meg. Meg swore me to secrecy when I saw the angry red marks all over her little sister's skin. On another visit, when I did not see Jeannie at all, I asked Meg where she was. She told me that her mother had put Jeannie in the basement because she had wet herself. When I asked how long had Jeannie had been in the basement, Meg's response was, "Five days."

Meg told me that her mother had been reported to the children's protection agency twice for her physical abuse of Jeannie. But each time they came to investigate, Mrs. Jones passed off a friend's child who was Jeannie's age as her daughter, telling the agency worker that whomever reported her was just trying to make trouble, and she could see for herself that her child showed no evidence of maltreatment. I think Mrs. Jones made her children suffer because she was angry that her husband had divorced her.

Years later, after Meg graduated from high school, she ran away from her mother and went to went to live with her father in another state. I remember late one Sunday afternoon I answered our doorbell to find Meg at my door. She wanted me to go to her mother's house and ask her sister for Meg's high school diploma, which she needed to register for college. Meg was clearly still deathly afraid of her mother, so I did as she asked and went to her mother's house, and Jeannie gave me Meg's diploma.

Sharing a similar home life was a bond for Meg and me. We spent a lot of time together at school, and on the phone after school. We both endured harsh family situations, and knowing the other was there made it more bearable until we found a way to escape. For Meg, that escape came when she moved to her father's house, and for me, it came with my marriage. But that would all come later.

My life went on, and I endured the nightmare of my existence by employing strategies of avoidance, prayer, or simply hiding under the covers. When I was older, I moved to the back bedroom to remove myself further from the noise and carnage.

Things remained the same between my parents—constant conflict, either verbal or physical. As a young attractive couple, their friends included them in most of their social activities, and they were always out in the evenings and on weekends, either together or separately. All of this social activity provided many opportunities for the green-eyed monster of jealousy to raise its head. And it usually did.

My mother was stylish, and I was proud of the way she dressed. Fashion meant everything to her. I can't remember her ever wearing or even owning a pair of flat shoes until very late in her life. Her feet were shod in high heels from morning until night. It seems strange now, in a time when most people dress so casually, that my mother was dressed up every morning in a lovely dress—she never wore pants—and in her high heel shoes. She had an outgoing personality that made her stand out in a crowd—sometimes too much if she was drinking. Whenever she stepped into a party, she would announce, "All you men, get your hands out of your pockets, your butts off your chairs, and grab someone to dance. This is a party!"

Although my mother had an outgoing personality, she didn't have any close girlfriends, and was something of a solitary figure. She usually went out alone if she was not with my father. Her only real interests seem to be centered on drinking and dancing. She didn't have any other hobbies. My father on the other hand, was a joiner, and had many male friends with whom he shared his love of fishing, card playing, and attending Philadelphia Phillies baseball games, where I was his constant companion.

In a sense, this made them an odd couple. My mother loved her liquor, but my father never took a drop, not even a beer. She loved to dance but he had two left feet. He had many friends and interests; my mother had few.

I was the tie that bound them, but even parentally they differed. My father loved to spend time with me, taking me with him to visit relatives and friends but my mother only took me with her when there was no option. My father was loving and supportive of me while my mother only criticized and found fault with me.

When my mother was drinking, which was often, she would find excuses to pick on me. Our encounters would go like this—she would return home around 10pm, and find me in the living room watching television. She would stroll up to the mantel place, brush her hair back, and stare at herself in the mirror for a couple of minutes. Then she would then turn to face me with a barrage of questions.

"Did you eat? Did you do the dishes? Did you put out the trash? Did you do your homework?" (I was in high school).

Each time I answered in the affirmative, she would continue until a question elicited a "No". The negative response would be the catalyst, and she would begin attacking me.

"You are just like your father, no good, selfish, vain, and you never do what you are supposed to do."

"Mother, please leave me alone," I'd tell her. "I am watching television."

Ignoring this, she would continue her assault. After a while, when I could take it no longer, I would erupt.

"I HATE YOU!" I would shout, running up the stairs to my bedroom, where I would slam the door as hard as I could. Interestingly, she never followed me.

I don't know how her own mother treated her, or if she was subject to the same kind of abuse. But my mother never hugged me nor offered words of encouragement, ever. When I was in my teens, I overheard her tell a friend that I never lied to her. To this day, I'm still not sure if this was a compliment or merely a disclosure. The only compliment from her I can remember came when I was well into my thirties. One evening, as we talked, I said something about myself, which must have annoyed her. She responded, "You have a cute face, but so what?" It was left-handed but it struck me like a full fist to the face. And the pain never ended. As a result, to this day it is very important for me to have friends and relatives show me that they appreciate me by acknowledging my accomplishments or contributions. The absence of my mother's affirmations left a mark. The fact that I can recite every compliment anyone has ever given to me testifies to this deprivation.

As horribly as my mother treated me, I know that my father's treatment of her was far worse. But even then, their inflicting damage on each other was reciprocal. One thing I could never make sense of is why my mother would dress up and go to a nightclub or a party without my father, knowing he was jealous and violent. Often when she returned, if he was home, he would fly into a rage; jerking her clothes from the closet, pushing her out the door with her clothes piled on top of her, all the while calling her the most insulting and vile names. And truth be told, when my father came home from being out without my mother, the scenario reversed itself. My mother would wait up and attack him the second he entered the house. Instead of throwing his clothes at him, she hurled accusations—naming some woman she thought he was seeing. If she assaulted him, things rapidly escalated. Neither of them ever held back or backed down.

This behavior didn't end with my childhood. Sadly, years later after I'd become a mother, my children witnessed the same horror when they stayed with my parents. I only learned of this recently when out of the blue my youngest son, who is now over forty, called and told me he had been abused as a child.

"When?" I asked. "Where?" "Who?"

He couldn't answer immediately because he was sobbing. After he composed himself, he told me he witnessed my father fighting my mother, hitting her with his fist and knocking her down. He said my father looked at him as if to say, *what are you going to do about it?*

"Mom," he told me, "I was a little kid, there was nothing I could do to help grandma."

I think my son's pain came from feelings of guilt because he could not protect his grandmother. Hearing this from him broke my heart. I had left my children unprotected from the same madness that I experienced.

What I learned? Children don't tell you when they are suffering, and they can and do carry the pain into adulthood.

Chapter
Two

*W*HEN I WAS STILL young, my father got seriously involved with a woman, and left my mother. After he left, her drinking grew even worse. And though my father returned to my mother five months later, she never got over his leaving her, and remained a broken and dejected woman for most of her life. Her personality changed. She was suspicious and angry all the time, pouncing on him for any small transgression, like talking to another woman or not coming home when she expected him. And she constantly reminded him of his betrayal. My father eventually gave up trying to get my mother to forgive and forget or to appease her. He preferred the company of friends or like-minded partiers, and was seldom home. In time my mother became a full-blown alcoholic, downing her sorrows by emptying her glass.

The more my mother drank, the more aggressive she was towards me. She was angry and unhappy, and I was her scapegoat. Lashing out and criticizing me for some infraction I didn't even know I had committed seemed to console her in some weird way. Nevertheless, I felt sorry for her, and would tell her to forget about my father, that she should look for someone—or something—that brought her joy. My making these suggestions infuriated her even more. She would respond by calling me all kinds of bad names.

Her favorite was, "You are just a prissy-ass gal. What can you tell me? You are selfish just like your father."

Not caring about me must have made it easier for my mother to make me the récipient of her anger. I don't think my mother ever loved me. When I was young, she would leave me in the care of a negligent neighbor, who would return to her own apartment leaving me unattended in ours. Sometimes I woke up in the middle of the night alone—fearing that my parents had been killed or had abandoned me. I eventually made a conscious decision to stop loving them. I am amazed that at this young age, I had the instinct to know that my survival depended on my not loving them.

Being the only child with no siblings, I felt lonely and loveless. My only companions were sadness, worry, and apprehension. This feeling of unease followed me even when I went to visit our neighbors. Unbeknownst to me, my mother had fought with someone in that family. For now she stayed drunk, and when she was drunk she would often start a fight with anyone over anything, and these neighbors would give me a chilly reception.

I was confused by their cold behavior towards me because like many of my parents' friends our neighbors came from the same small town in Georgia, and in a sense were like family, warm and welcoming. While the men worked, most of the women spent their day's playing cards, Bid Whist or some other game—stopping only when it was time to rush home and prepare dinner. When my mother was drinking, which was often, she was argumentative and belligerent, and would invariably disrupt the card game by accusing someone of cheating. More and more, she ceased to be included, and replaced those lost friends with new drinking buddies.

In our house, things went from bad to worse, especially when my mother agreed to take care of her sister's two young children. My Aunt Mary, who lived in New York, asked my mother to keep her two young daughters for three months while she and her husband settled into a new home and a new job. My cousins were babies—18 months and two and a half years old. I was still in elementary school and had to baby-sit every day after school so my mother could drink with her friends before it was time for my father to come home. For obvious reasons, this made me very angry! I felt she was abusing me by forcing me to baby-sit her nieces every day. My argument was that she was the one who volunteered to take the babies, so she should be the one to care for them.

I fought with my mother over this; I screamed and yelled at her that she was unfair.

"It was you who agreed to take care of these children!" I protested, following her around the apartment with the baby on my hip. "I want to go outside and play with my friends. I should not have to stay in and baby sit while you go off and drink with your friends."

Sometimes she would slap me when I spoke to her this way. But I still protested.

Three months turned into six, then nine. My aunt never came to see her children nor did she send money for their care. This became another bone of contention between my parents. When nine months had passed and there was no word from my aunt, my mother's parents, who lived in Georgia, agreed to take the children. A relative took the babies by train to Georgia, where they stayed with my grandparents for more than four years.

Eventually, my grandmother got fed up and took the kids, now six and seven years old, back to New York and returned them to their mother, my aunt. By this time, my aunt and her husband had divorced. I was told my aunt was none too happy when her mother returned those children to her care.

This was a very sad time both in my life and in the life of my parents. My father had returned to his old ways, and they continued fighting over my father's philandering and my mother's drinking. Adding insult to injury, my mother said my father was having an affair with someone she knew. I could hear them arguing about one woman and then another, people either real or imagined, it was anybody's best guess. My mother was jealous and miserable. I would tell myself that no one would ever treat me the way my father treated my mother, and it became one of my driving principles.

What I learned? Never love a man more than he loves you, or if you do, don't let him know it.

Chapter

Three

$\mathcal{S}$OME SUMMERS I GOT a reprieve from my parents when my cousin Ann would take me to visit my maternal grandparents, James and Annabelle Lowery and, other relatives in Georgia. I was very close to my grandparents. My grandfather, Jim, as they called him, was a very interesting man. He had very little formal education, but he was extremely well read. My Uncle Tom, his son, said Jim could converse on any subject from astronomy to epistemology, and had read the Bible completely. One of his part-time jobs was selling Black magazines and newspapers. The paper I remember was the Pittsburgh Courier. When I was visiting, he would tap me to go with my aunt to collect money from his customers. Sometimes when Aunt Helen and I approached people for payment, someone would say something like, "Tell Mr. Lowery, I will pay next week."

"Pay today, credit tomorrow," was always my response. My grandfather Jim got a big kick out of this. He'd say, "Pick Claudette, she *will* collect your money!"

There was one room in the house dedicated to my grandfather's books. He had several locks on the door, and we thought it a great privilege whenever we were allowed inside. It was a musty old room with shelves and shelves of books. The dim light made it kind of spooky. And even though I was unable to read and understand most of those books, I would choose one and carefully page through it, glad to be sharing this time with my grandfather Jim. My Aunt Helen, who was five years older than me, did not spend much time in my grandfather's library. So browsing through my grandfather's books, and asking him questions when he was not busy reading, made me feel a bit grown up, and kind of special. Grandfather Jim eventually lost his sight and went totally blind. This was very sad for a person who loved to read. My grandmother said he lost his sight from all that reading in very dim light. It seems kind of a cruel thing to say, especially given that we now know he lost his sight because of glaucoma.

Everyone called my grandmother Toolie. She was beautiful, had a great wit, and seemed to stay forever young. One of my proudest memories of her was when I was around four and a man asked her, "Toolie is that your young'un?"

"No," Grandmother Toolie replied, "that's my grandbaby."

"Well, she looks just like you," the man said.

I once asked my grandmother when did men stop running around? "When they are dead," she answered, wryly.

Many years later while she was visiting with me, a few of my girlfriends stopped by our house early one morning. They had been up all night partying, and they were using a lot of curse words in their conversation. I was concerned my grandmother would be offended. But after my friends left, her only comment was, "those girls really know how to have a good time." Toolie was not judgmental, and never took sides when she spent time visiting with her married children.

I only met my father's parents, Watson Hodges and Emma Cooper, one time. I remember Grandmother Toolie telling me that my Grandmother Emma, had five beautiful children, my father being one. Although I only met my grandfather Watson once, I know a lot about his family history. His father, Thomas Hodges, was the first black person in the area to receive an inheritance. His father, a former slave, left him 16 acres of land upon his death around the 1870's. Thomas Watson donated a portion of this land to build a church, Hodges Grove.

The church is still serving its congregation and the community today. Very recently, his youngest daughter, Vonzie Dansby, who lived to be 98 and spent most of her adult life in Ohio, died, and her funeral was in the same church her father had built so many decades earlier.

Attending my 98-year-old aunt's funeral in a church that was founded and built by her father, and with almost every solitary soul in the pews also a relative (including the female preacher), was an otherworldly experience for me. I felt like I was wrapped in a cocoon of love tied with an umbilical cord of history.

My grandfather Watson's mother, Chloe Love, also had a a very unique family history. We are all fortunate that a cousin was able to trace Chloe Love's family all the way back to 1810, when they belonged to a slave owner named Andrew Donaldson. Donaldson had several children by his slaves, and one of them was Dora Donaldson, whose descendants worked with other former slaves to found a school for Black children in Portal, Georgia. The school, which occupied an old turpentine shanty with just one small stove to heat it, is said to have been the first learning institution for Black children in the area. The students were taught by 15-year-old Georgiana Riggs, herself a former slave who had secretly learned both to read and write when she was still a slave—a "crime" that could be punishable by death for student and teacher alike. The school, Willow Hill, survives to this day. It is now named the Willow Hill Heritage and Renaissance Center, and operates in collaboration with the Georgia Southern University on The Willow Hill Digital Archive Project to preserve the history of the school and the area. Dr. Alvin Jackson, an alumnus and a descendant of Dora Donaldson, was the historian and is currently the chairman of the board of the Willow Hill Heritage and Renaissance Center.

As a child, I was unaware of my family's history, and I just enjoyed visiting and being with my relatives. Life in Georgia was completely different from life in Philadelphia. There was freedom from stress, freedom to roam and to play all day without a worry or care. There was no one arguing or fighting; no one angry or sad, just a lot of open spaces to explore and new adventures to experience.

My Uncle John, who also lived in Georgia, had a farm. He also had thirteen children—one boy and twelve girls. Farmers and their wives often had large families, and it was commonplace for the older children to help their parents work the land and raise the livestock. When I was visiting with my grandparents, my uncle John and his wife aunt May would invite me to spend one or two weeks with them on their farm. I soon discovered what life on a farm was really like. Everyone had to get up at 5:30 in the morning. We would eat breakfast, then begin the day doing chores, first feeding the animals and then off to the field where we either picked cotton or pulled tobacco. Picking cotton by hand was hard work. You had to reach into the plant and pick the soft cotton from the boll, which was covered in prickers. The sun was hot, the thorns on the bolls would scratch your fingers, and there was always the chance that a rattlesnake might bite you. By the end of the day, I was exhausted but thrilled to be sharing this work with my cousins.

They promised to pay me for my work, but I never saw any money. Thinking back, I should have paid them for the fun and joy I had. Living on a farm was, for me, like living in a fantasy world. When I wanted grapes, I pulled them from the vine. If I wanted peanuts, I dug them from the ground. If I wanted watermelon, I snapped one off at the stem. Nothing in the world tastes as good as food you've just picked with your own hands. This was thrilling for a city kid who had only seen and tasted these items in a grocery store.

I'm sure my cousins didn't share my feelings of joy and excitement in picking cotton or pulling tobacco. Living on a farm was hard work. The animals had to be fed, the crop had to be brought in on time and there was always new planting to be done. But I didn't know any of this. I just relished in the freedom and fun of being in this moment of peace and tranquility. Eating dinner with my cousins and their parents was an adventure in and of itself. The first time I dined at the farm I was amazed, for I had never seen so much food on a table for just a regular meal. There were huge bowls of corn, green beans, rice, and stewed tomatoes; as well as platters of fried chicken, ham and beef, along with hot biscuits, and corn bread. Farming was hard work and you built up a huge appetite. By the end of the day, everyone was starving, eager to rush to the table and dig in to devour the hearty feast.

Sitting around the farm table, everyone talked about the events of the day. It was wondrous for me to witness the warmth and camaraderie between each family member. They teased and joked and shared funny stories accumulated during the day. They quickly included me in this web of family warmth, so completely opposite of what I experienced in my own home. It was obvious that my uncle still loved my aunt, even after all those children, and that their children loved each other. Here I witnessed mother and father hugging, and kids laughing and kidding each other. No one was angry, even when they had extra chores to do, or someone took their straw hat and they had to pick cotton in the sun without the shade of the brim that would keep sunburn from one's neck.

Although they thought I was strange because I talked funny, and I never stopped asking questions—"Where did this come from?" "Where do you go to school?" "How do you plant these vegetables?"—hey tolerated my curiosity with love and patience. I kept the memories of those farm visits close to my heart for a lifetime.

The kids' ages ranged from age one to eighteen. At the time, I was still a preteen yet they all treated me as if I was their age no matter which cousin I was with. There was so much to share with my friends when I returned to Philadelphia at the end of those summers. I told them about my exciting adventures, the amazing meals, and especially my working on the farm. I liked how impressed my friends were when they learned I did real farm work just like my cousins.

What I learned? There are families who love each other and are brought closer when working with the soil and the animals that sustain their lives.

Chapter

Four

*W*HEN WE ARE YOUNG, childhood seems to go on forever. Unfortunately, if a childhood is an unhappy one, it can seem to go on twice as long. This was my experience—drawn out days, weeks, months and years, enduring the harness of my mother's ill treatment and the sadness of being a witness to her unhappiness. There are probably many variables involved in surviving a troubled childhood. One factor might simply be a product of nature. There is a saying, "Some children are born like glass. If you hit them, they shatter. Others are born like plastic. If you hit them, they bend. Still others are born like steel, you strike them, and you only leave a scar." I think I was born like steel, because I was able to survive my mother's anger and abuse and still kindle the hope that I would have a happier life.

Over the years our family dynamics remained unchanged and I continued to maintain an emotional distance from my parents. I did whatever worked, and for the most part that meant pretending not to care, avoiding them when I could, and escaping as soon as an opportunity presented itself. After I did escape and took control of my life, I was always kind to them, but I never removed the cloak of my emotional protection.

What I learned? When love hurts, you need to love people from a distance—either physical or emotional, or both.

Chapter
Five

*Y*EARS AGO, PEOPLE WERE not as aware as they are today of the threats children faced from bullies, abusive parents, or child molesters. So my parents and other parents in my neighborhood were unaware of a monster in our midst. Our neighbor Mr. Bill, was elderly, white, single, and always very kind to everyone. As it turned out, he was also a pedophile. When I was nine years old I met Mr. Bill through the other kids on my block. He was a photographer, and would often invite the neighborhood kids to his home for candy and other treats, where had them pose for pictures. He spent hours taking pictures of us dressed in the many costumes he had in his large wardrobe of props. Mr. Bill seemed to adore kids, and we had great fun dressing up and taking pictures as Indians, cowboys, ballerinas, soldiers, policemen, or clowns—whatever was our fantasy.

Sometimes Mr. Bill allowed us into his dark room to help him develop the photos he took of us. We were delighted and thrilled to do this and it made us feel very special. He also enthralled us with stories of his foreign travels and his exotic adventures. He had pictures of himself climbing mountains in Asia, catching large fish in the Bahamas, and rafting down rivers. We would sit at his feet, our eyes stretched wide, mouths open—listening as he regaled us with his escapades. He never seemed to tire of us, and we were always welcome and we could choose to eat anything we wanted from his basket of treats. I remember feeling so sure we were the envy of other kids when we told them about Mr. Bill, and all the fun we had with him.

A few years later, our entire neighborhood was shocked when they read in the newspaper that Mr. Bill was arrested for molesting a child. The paper stated that he had molested many children during the years he was our neighbor. The police had a great deal of damning evidence from the photographs he had taken, and from the testimonies of his victims. Our parents were stunned that this good looking, seemingly kind, elderly, gentleman was the same person they read about in the newspaper. Although, Mr. Bill never molested me, I am now convinced he took pictures of us as we undressed and changed into our costumes. I can't remember the outcome of Mr. Bill's trial, or if he went to prison, but someone told me that he died on the street coming home from shopping. Probably shopping for candy to give to some unsuspecting child.

What I learned? Parents need to pay close attention when any adults spend time with their children.

Chapter

Six

*E*VEN THOUGH IT TURNED out we had a pedophile living in our midst, everyone still felt safe, because it was a close-knit community where all the neighbors knew each other, and watched out for each other. If you were out after dark, a grown up would tell you to go home, or ask a series of questions if they thought you were up to doing something wrong. But as time passed, the neighborhood changed—families moved away, and new people moved in and disrupted the sense of community. When I was 13, a new family moved in with some kids who were about my age. They were what people used to call bad kids because they fought, cursed and smoked. One day they asked, and I agreed to play hooky from school with them. Initially, I wanted to say "no", but I felt a bit intimidated, and didn't want to get on their wrong side—they were tough and I feared they might beat me up if I didn't go along.

There were five of us indulging in truancy that day. We played hooky at a house belonging to a girl named Debby, even though she had gone to school. I could tell these kids had done this before because they climbed in the basement window and let the rest of us into the house. I was petrified the whole day, fearing that Debby's mother might come home and call the police. I couldn't wait until the time for school to be out, so we could leave the house.

To avoid being put in this vulnerable position again, the very next morning I forged a letter from my mother to my junior high school

21

principal. The letter explained that we had moved, and requested that the school transfer me to a school in my new district. I gave him the address of a friend who lived in that district, and he approved it. I told my mother the school transferred me to Fitzsimmons Junior High School because it was a better school, and would be better suited to my intelligence. She never questioned it, and ironically, a year later my parents purchased a house in that school district. The new school was more interesting and challenging academically, and that was where I began writing poetry to express my sadness and loneliness.

What I learned? Sometimes children are forced to be proactive in solving their own problems.

Chapter

Seven

𝒻ITZSIMMONS JUNIOR HIGH WAS more racially and economically diverse than my previous school. Over sixty percent of the students at Fitzsimmons were white. Up until then, I had attended school with a student body that was composed mostly of Black students and Black teachers. For the first time, I felt overwhelmed by another student's intelligence, and it was at Fitzsimmons that I experienced my first put-down.

It was near Halloween, and I flippantly asked one of my classmates, "Why are you wearing that ugly mask?" as I gestured to his face.

"I am practicing," he shot back. "What's your excuse?"

I was clearly out-matched.

In our Honors English class, our first assignment was to write a composition introducing ourselves. Most of the students' compositions were similar, comprised just of their name, where they lived, and if they had sibling. But one student chose to use a hypothetical one-way telephone conversation to tell us about herself.

"Hi Jim. Nice to meet you," she wrote. "My name is Carol, what would you like to know about me?"

I considered her brilliant to come up with such a clever and creative way of introducing herself. I didn't think I could compete with such brilliance. It never occurred to me that someone might have given her the idea and therefore perhaps she was not so excessively brilliant after all.

What I learned? Don't take things at face value. Sometimes they are not what they seem.

Chapter
Eight

$\mathscr{B}$Y THE END OF my first year of junior high school my mother had become a complete alcoholic. Drunk most of the time, she directed her wrath towards me when my father was not there to receive it. When he did come home, they'd engage in their usual altercations, the fighting sometimes spilling outside of the house. I was especially ashamed of the scenes my mother caused with the neighbors watching. Some unkind people even teased me about it, which made me feel really bad, and impacted my self-esteem. In spite of the chaos at home, my junior high school years were mostly fun.

I was smart and popular. My friends and I participated in school activities together—reading, social studies, and glee club. My involvement in the glee club was a standing joke among my friends because I can't carry a tune. But the glee club was fun, and we didn't have to audition, so no one knew I could not sing. It was just another opportunity to be with my friends. Like most teenagers, we liked to spend as much time together as possible, and never tired of each other's company.

During the winter we went to dances, and in the summer we went on picnics. This was when I learned to play pinochle—one of Philadelphia's favorite card games, and a skill required of everyone in my neighborhood. I learned to be a very good player. The proof that you're good is when someone invites you to be his or her partner. All in all, this was a good period in my life.

My having fun and being popular did not please my mother. Maybe misery does love company? In any case the following incident gives a glimpse into how my mother showed her displeasure when things were going too well for me.

I was chosen to be a speaker at my junior high school graduation. Even though my mother bought me lots of clothes, she absolutely refused to buy me a new dress for my graduation. I felt certain my mother's refusal to get me a new dress for this special occasion was for no other purpose than to be mean to me. My suspicions were confirmed when a close friend offered to buy me a dress—and mother gave a flat out "no" to the offer.

"Claudette has lots of dresses," she said to my friend in a tight voice, "and she can wear one of them to her graduation."

I was extremely disappointed because I loved clothes and having a new dress for my graduation was important to me. My mother added insult to injury by refusing to attend the graduation, telling me to take her sister, Sarah, who was visiting with us. By this time, I had learned to speak up for myself.

"I am your only child," I said to her. "I am graduating and have been honored to be a speaker at the graduation, and my own mother doesn't want to attend? HOW DO YOU THINK I CAN EVER AMOUNT TO ANYTHING?"

After that, she agreed to go. But it didn't make me feel good because I had to shame my own mother into attending my graduation.

Things went downhill from there. I was nervous, and said my speech far too quickly. After we returned home from the graduation, my mother spent the rest of that day and the next two weeks criticizing my performance and comparing me to my best friend Meg, who had delivered a stunning speech. My mother was very dramatic. She did not only tell you something, she acted it out. Admittedly, I was nervous and spoke too quickly, and maybe some criticism was warranted, but not three-weeks-worth. My mother never seemed to tire of it. She would stand as if she were at the podium, and repeat the first three lines of Meg's speech, or as much of the speech as she could remember.

Then she'd say, "Claudette you spoke too fast and no one could understand what you were saying. But Meg, she gave her speech perfectly! 'The youth of today are our leaders of tomorrow.'"

She imitated Meg's gestures, stamping her feet and slamming down her fist to emphasize an important point in the speech, just as Meg had done. This demonstration would go on until she exhausted the lines she remembered—all the while pointing out how terribly I had delivered my speech.

Both Meg and I had mothers who treated us horribly. My mother wouldn't buy me a new dress for graduation, but Meg's mother made her wear one of her own old dresses that was four sizes too large for Meg. Poor Meg, she had altered the dress by hand to make it fit and it looked awful.

Meg was a pretty girl, and she was ashamed of how she looked. Before her speech, she began shaking and had to be removed from the stage, taken to the nurse's office, and given a sedative. Not to take anything away from Meg, but that medication might explain why she was so calm. She recited her speech with confidence and passion. The ill-treatment by our mothers was a bond that connected us. Oddly, in spite of how badly my mother treated me, she nonetheless loved Meg. And Meg was the standard by which my mother measured me during my mid-teens, always making comparisons where I came up short. Surprisingly, I never felt envy or anger towards Meg and I love her to this day.

With my mother constantly putting me down at every opportunity, it took years and a lot of effort before I realized I was a good person, and that she was wrong to say such negative things about me. At least, she was wrong about most of them.

Many years later, after my second marriage, my close friend Shirley called me after leaving an appointment her therapist. She had also been having problems with her mother. She said her therapist told her that her mother didn't experience her as her daughter, but as a sister with whom she competed. She knew my situation with my mother and asked if my mother had sisters.

"Yes," I said. "Four, but the only sister she would compete with would be her sister Sarah." Sarah was the one she told me to take to my junior high school graduation.

Shirley told me to call my mother and ask her whom of her sisters I was most like.

So I called my mother. When she answered, I asked, "Mother, who I am most like out of all your sisters?"

Without a moment's hesitation, she answered, "Sarah."

I asked why and she said, "Sarah was outgoing, and liked to meet people, but Mary was sincere, and loved the family."

I later learned that there is often conflict between mothers and daughters. Sometimes it happens when the mother is beautiful and the daughter is not, and the mother experiences disappointment. Other times the daughter is nice-looking and the mother is not, and this causes the mother to have envy. The problems between my mother and me might be attributed to many things, one being that my father spoiled me —he never said no when I asked him for something, nor did he let my mother discipline me if he was present. But he ignored her. Even with the pain my mother brought me, I still had a lot of sympathy for her. She was an attractive and talented woman, and she had the most beautiful singing voice. She sounded like Sarah Vaughan and Billie Holiday combined. When she was older and had given up drinking, friends and relatives often asked her to sing at family occasions, something she seemed to enjoy. My mother really missed her calling. She should have been a performer.

In a sense, she was. As I mentioned earlier, she was very dramatic and would act out and dramatize any story she was telling, in such a way that made you feel as if you were right there. The scene I remember most is her telling the story of her brother who was a basketball player and wanted to leave class early to attend practice, and the response his teacher gave him. I can see her now, describing how great a basketball player her brother Tom was. You could see the imaginary ball in her hand and her standing on the foul line. She would then pretend to release the ball, just as her brother would have done. The imaginary ball would go into the imaginary net, thereby, winning the game. Still standing, she'd recite the words of Tom's teacher.

"Yes, Mr. Lowery, I understand you are a basketball star and you want to leave my class early so you can go to practice. But, Mr. Lowery, I am a teacher, and you are also a student and this is my class. If you wish to leave this class early and go to practice, you are going to have to go through me."

My mother would imitate how the teacher looked blocking the door and how her brother, with a look of defeat, went back to his desk and sat down until the class was over.

She was a very talented woman, but her demons prevented her from enjoying her gifts or being kind to me. Sometimes her unkindness was not only deliberate, but cruel. Once, when I was fifteen, I confided in her that I had a crush on a neighbor. It was my first crush.

Two days after I shared this with her, she told me she had gone to visit the boy's family and told him, "My daughter really likes you. Don't make a fool out of her."

I felt betrayed, and was so angry with her that I didn't speak to her for days. The boy was four years older than I was and didn't take my crush seriously. He just teased me a lot, sometimes taking things from me until I begged for him to give them back. His callous treatment didn't feel good. I was at a disadvantage because he knew about my crush on him, and took advantage. This was a learning experience for me, and I vowed to never again like any man more than they liked me.

Chapter

Nine

*D*URING THIS TIME, MY father was in the background. Up until I was 13, I was his buddy. He took me to Philadelphia Phillies' baseball games, even the double-headers, and to the holiday parades—both the Thanksgiving and the Mummers parades. He also took me to see Santa Claus, and bought most of my clothes when I was little. One experience remains vivid in my memory. It was a Sunday afternoon. I think it was Easter Sunday, and we had gone to church. After the service, he took me to the drug store and bought me a strawberry milkshake. At the time, they made the shakes in a metal container—they probably still do. I was around six, and the waitress gave me the entire contents of the container. I can feel my stomach now growing full, as I continued to pull on the straw until I had drained the entire milkshake. But when I was 13, this easy camaraderie all changed and my father stopped interacting with me. He just removed himself. I didn't understand it at the time. Now I think maybe it was because I was becoming a young woman and he did not know how to deal with it. I missed being his buddy, even though he continued to spoil me—giving me anything I asked after I wore him down. These interactions with my father provided the training I needed later to become a successful fund-raiser—never accept the first, second or third "no."

Even my mother acknowledged that my father was a good provider. He took good care of us in terms of providing a nice home, and buying all the material things we needed. My girlfriend Barbara accused me of being spoiled, and getting everything I wanted from both of my parents. This was partly true, if you were looking from the outside. But kids need more than material things, they need security and stability, and this was missing from my life.

My father belonged to a number of organizations—the Masons, a poker group and "Club 15," a social group for Black men. My teenage girlfriends frequently commented on how handsome the 15 members of my father's club were. The Club held two events each year; a semi-formal dance in the winter and a picnic on the New Jersey Shore in the summer. When I turned 16, I was allowed to attend both affairs. I loved to dance, I still do. At the summer picnic, I would dance until I was wet with perspiration. My father would come over to ask me to sit down and take a rest. But I wanted to dance every dance. I still cherish those fun times.

I also remember the first time I had an experience that triggered my suspicion that men bear considerable watching. I was 16 and had just gotten my driving learner's permit. My father was hosting his poker group in our dining room. I had asked him earlier when was he going to take me driving, because he had put me off several times. I was excited and wanted to get more practice before my next driving school lesson. So I interrupted him and asked him again. Ignoring me, he placed a bid. I didn't leave and was very persistent. It was then that his friend Fred volunteered to come by the next Saturday and take me driving. This satisfied me and I left them to their game.

Sure enough, Fred showed up in his red convertible Buick at noon. He asked where I wanted to go to practice. I said Fairmount Park, which is a large inner city park in Philadelphia. Once we entered the park he let me take the wheel. After I started to drive, he started calling me pretty and saying I looked like "a convertible girl." He offered to take me driving anytime. I knew then that he was a jerk, if not a predator. Fairmount Park is adjacent to the Schuylkill River and Rock Creek Parkway. The parkway is a very curvy road, and the cars on it tend to drive very fast. Once on the parkway there is no place to exit for miles. I decided Fred needed to be taught a lesson and drove the car onto Rock Creek Parkway. This was only my third driving lesson; the first two were at school. I told him this as the cars sped by us—blowing their horns because I was driving too slowly.

I was frightened but I exaggerated my fear.

"Oh, I am scared, what should I do?" I exclaimed. "I can't slow down because the cars are too close behind us."

The horns were loud. I looked at Fred and he was sweating and appeared to be in shock. No one was ever more relieved than he was, when I could turn off the parkway and he could take the wheel. When I returned home I told my father about my behavior and Fred's reaction. But I left out the part about him making a pass at me. My father said his fear was related to the fact that it was not his car, but his girlfriend's. I don't remember seeing Fred at our house again. I can't say I was sorry at his absence.

Chapter
Ten

$\mathcal{L}$ATER MY VIEW THAT men bear considerable watching received further confirmation, after an incident that happened when I was 16, and at home in my bed. As was her custom, my mother was entertaining her drinking friends in our kitchen. I had come home around 10 p.m., on this particular evening, and had gone into the kitchen to say hello to her friends and good night to my mother. They were all sitting around the kitchen table drinking, and talking—two women, including my mother, and two men.

Our kitchen, dining room, and living room were all on the ground floor; the bedrooms and bathrooms were on the second and third floors. After leaving my mother and her friends, I went to my bedroom on the second floor, undressed and went to bed. Sometime later, I awoke to find someone sitting on my bed. It was a man.

"Don't holler," the man whispered.

At first I thought it was someone playing a joke, so I said, "Okay, I'm not going to holler.

"Holler and die," he said. Then he pulled my bedcovers down to my knees.

I knew this was no joke, and I jumped up, screaming at the top of my voice.

"MOTHERRRR!" I shouted.

My mother and her friends ran up the stairs into my room asking what happened. I told them that a man had tried to get in my bed, and had run into the bathroom when I started screaming. They all went to the bathroom door, and called for him to come out. He didn't come out immediately—they could hear him jiggling the toilet handle. When he did finally emerge, they were waiting for him with a lot of curse words and threats. They chased him out of the house. My mother knew him well, but I didn't; he was our neighbor's brother. Under different circumstances, this could have been very serious. As it was it was, it was very frightening.

What I learned? Many men are hunters—hunting for opportunities for sexual encounters. And some men are predators, looking for prey. Girls and women need to be aware of this, even with men they know. Although I was now aware that some men could not be trusted, I was not aware enough. I suffered another incident when I was in my twenties that did not turn out as well.

Chapter

Eleven

$\mathcal{M}$Y LIFE BEGAN TO change for the better when I was in my teens and in high school. This was the time I became very close to my Aunt Willie. She was my father's sister and someone I turned to for advice and counsel. She also ran interference between my mother and me. She would explain to my mother what teenage girls were like and what they needed and enjoyed, including why it was normal and reasonable for me to want a new dress for a big school dance. In spite of the fact that it was my senior prom, once again, my mother refused to give me money to buy a gown. To her credit, she had given me the money earlier and I had spent it on school clothes, telling her I didn't want to go to mine because I had gone with someone else to his prom the year before. Hearing my friends talk about their dresses and the plans for the after-prom parties changed my mind. Now I did want to go, but my mother refused to give me more money, and I refused to wear the gown I had worn as a prom date the year before.

This is when my Aunt Willie stepped in to support me knowing I had spent the money my mother gave me on other clothes. She knew I was spoiled, and should not have expected my mother to give me more money to buy a prom gown. None of this mattered to her. In the end, she bought me a dress herself. It was a long, white chiffon gown, and it took my date's breath away. All of my friends rushed up to tell me how much they loved my dress and how beautiful it was. Most of the girls had short prom dresses, and my long dress stood out. This was the impression I wanted to make, and it added to my reputation for being the best-dressed girl in my class. It is sad for me to tell you that my mother was not home the night of my prom to help me get ready. One of our neighbors came over to help me dress, and called my Aunt Willie to come and see me before I left for the prom. My mother happened to stop by my aunt's house latter that night, and everyone criticized her harshly for not being home to help me dress for my prom. I used to blame my mother's neglecting me on her drinking, but now I suspect she did not want to celebrate any of my achievements.

My Aunt Willie was my guardian angel. She made me feel special, spent a lot of time with me, and spoiled me like my father. She was someone I trusted with my secrets. She also rescued me from my mother's constant criticism, when she was around, explaining to her what it was like to be young and carefree. Willie was a beautiful and wise woman. Being my mentor she taught me many important lessons about life in general—and about men in particular. Her message was to "always place a high value on you. What men get cheaply, they value cheaply."

After the experience of being twice divorced, Aunt Willie knew a lot about men and about life, and she had many nuggets of wisdom to share, such as, "many women spend time making themselves beautiful. That's good, but it is equally important to make yourself interesting. You can do this by listening to others and by reading the newspapers every day. If you read the newspapers every day, you will know what is going on in the world and you can have an intelligent conversation with anyone."

I thought if I equipped myself with these attributes that I'd have a good chance at having a good life.

Tall and elegant, my aunt had many admirers. I always thought she resembled Dorothy Dandridge, the movie actress. She was single, independent and confident, and wanted to make me in her image.

As my mentor, Aunt Willie dispensed advice on almost every subject possible. I was an enthusiastic student and listened attentively whenever my aunt shared her knowledge with me. She told me to always be my own person, not to be a follower, and to always chart my own course. She told me told to make myself attractive, both inside and out, because on the whole, attractive people have more opportunities, are judged less harshly and have easier lives. I took her messages to heart, pledging that I would be as attractive as possible, as kind as possible, as intelligent as possible, and as interesting as possible.

My aunt was both kind and generous. And she exposed me to her world of glamour. Watching her as she interacted with her lovely female friends and handsome suitors was captivating. I enjoyed listening to their conversations as they shared stories about their parties, their dates and their many adventures out on the town. I loved looking at their striking pictures—women in their gorgeous gowns, the men in their tails and white ties. They were Black and fabulous. This was the 1950's, before integration, and black people had their own exclusive nightclubs. My aunt was dating a man I think was the love of her life, Joe Harris. He was suave, charming, and the source of the elegant white tie parties. He was affiliated with one of the upscale Black nightclubs where my aunt and her friends were patrons. I am sure this is how they met. My father would never wear tails to the parties, but he *would* wear a tuxedo. They reflected elegance and sophistication, and these images made a vivid impression on me that has lasted a lifetime.

Aunt Willie shared a two-story home with my Aunt Pearlie. They were both divorced, and the house was always full of people enjoying one another's company—from the living room through the dining room and into the kitchen. Willie always had lots of food and lots of things to drink on hand. She was popular and the leader in her group of friends. She was always the life of the party— quick to laugh. There was never a quiet moment in her presence. She was usually planning a party, attending a party, or leaving a party, many times calling in the middle of the night for someone to come and fetch her, when she was unable to procure a cab to take her home. When I got older, I was the one she often called for a ride.

Willie had a childhood friend named Ida. She was also Willie's roommate. Willie had a lot of influence over Ida and could talk her into just about anything. For example, one time Willie talked Ida into going on an expensive bus tour. Ida didn't want to go because she didn't want to spend the money. But Willie persisted and insisted, until Ida gave in and purchased her ticket. They had to get up very early the morning of the bus tour to meet the bus. As was her custom, Willie had a party the night before the bus tour, so it was not surprising that they stayed up very late partying into the wee hours, and they both overslept.

The following morning, Willie entered Ida's room in a panic.

"Ida wake up, wake up," Willie exclaimed. "The bus has gone!"

"I know damn well that bus ain't gone," Ida declared.

Ida fussed all day saying she didn't want to go in the first place, the ticket was too expensive, and now all of her money was wasted because they missed the bus. She would not let Willie rest until finally Willie got someone to take them to meet the bus and join the group. Willie enjoyed telling the story of how funny Ida looked with her big eyes, a scarf tied around her head, and how she responded upon learning they had missed the bus.

She kept repeating Ida's words, "I know damn well that bus ain't gone."

Willie was always up to something fun. She had a lot of kid in her, loved to play, and enjoyed being with young people. She would be the first one to throw a snowball and if it hit you, she would laugh with delight. At my sweet sixteen birthday party, which she hosted and paid for, she involved herself in everything—creating the invitations, choosing the menu, and organizing the evening. I had 40 friends at my party, a mix of boys and girls from ages 15 to 18. We played games with the adults early in the evening, but after we ate, the kids moved the party to our basement, where one of the boys changed the light bulb from white to red. These were called red light parties. The most popular song of the night was "Earth Angel" by a young singing group called the Penguins. It was slow, steamy, and the kids danced very close when it played. My father came down one time to take a look, but he didn't stay, and we danced until twelve o'clock. Many of my girlfriends spent the night, and none of us got much sleep. We were so excited and replayed the evening over and over again during our conversations. I was mentoring a group of girls many years later and heard them playing this song. It bought back happy memories of my wonderful sweet sixteen party and the love I have for my Aunt Willie.

Willie was my father's sister, but she would never side with him against my mother. She knew he was a lousy husband—a philanderer. We both attributed my mother's drinking to my father's affairs with other women. My aunt was very understanding and kind to my mother, often inviting her to events just to get her out of the house, and her mind off my father. Willie knew how much my mother loved my father, and would tell me how when they were out at a club, and a man paid my mother some attention, she would quickly tell him she was married, showing him her wedding ring.

I stayed angry with my father for many years because of how he treated my mother, to the point that I never acknowledged, even to myself, that I was named after him. His name is Claude; my name is Claudette. Whenever I was asked about the origin of my name, I would say I was named after Claudette Corbett, my mother's favorite actress. When I was 36 years old, someone asked if I had French ancestry because Claudette was a French name.

"No," I said. "I am named after my father."

This hit me like a thunderbolt. I stood still for a long time, stunned. That memory is still with me. It is surprising how I never thought of this. Claude and Claudette. This revelation threw me. We were named as father and daughter. Wow—the power of repression!

Aunt Willie had one son, Howard, who was five years older than me, and was really like my big brother. Willie, Howard and I spent a lot of time together. The three of us would often go to matinee movies followed by dinner at a restaurant. It was exciting having Howard as my older brother. I was 15 during this time, and I could ask him anything and everything. I had many questions about boys and sex. Howard treated me like I was much older and he was the most special person to me. He shared secrets about his life: his girlfriends, his ambitions, and his fears. We also shared our thoughts and feelings about our mothers. Having a beautiful young single mother was troublesome for Howard, especially when it came to her boyfriends. His critiques of them, always negative, would result in a big fight between him and Aunt Willie. This was probably normal. Boys don't think anyone is good enough for their mothers.

Howard was handsome, like his mother was beautiful, and there was often conflict between them over his choice in women. My aunt was very upset when Howard dated women who were much older than he was. Like his mother, he was intelligent, interesting, and fun. He would read all night and have trouble getting up for work in the mornings. This was another source of contention between them. After one of their big altercations, he moved out of his mother's house and in with my parents and me.

Here was another person who spoiled me. I went shopping for a leather coat, and had a hard time choosing between the black or red one. I bought the black one. But when I got home, I couldn't get over my desire for the red one. Well, Howard gave me the money so I went back later and bought the red one. I adored Howard; I think we adored each other. We were both Aquarius, and very compatible: we enjoyed the same things: music, people, and movies. Later, when I had children, they loved and enjoyed Howard as much as I did.

It wasn't surprising that most people wanted to be around Howard. He was smart, non-judgmental, charming, and had a great sense of humor. One day after he had overslept and went to work late, he returned from work early. I asked why he was home so early.

He said, "I am not going back until that man takes back what he said." Thinking he had called him a N-----, I asked "What did he say?" Howard responded, **"YOU ARE FIRED."**

I laughed long and hard because the answer was so unexpected. Howard attracted friends with wit and humor like himself. I remember him telling me a story about his best friend Bernard. Bernard stopped by his apartment late one night after winning a considerable amount of money playing poker. He was quite drunk and through all of the money on Howard's sofa. After a few more drinks, Bernard left for home.

Early the next morning Howard's phone rang. It was Bernard, "Man they got me, they ripped me off. Took all my money." Howard let Bernard commiserate a bit more, before he said. "Bernard, I have your money. You threw it on my sofa and it's still there." Bernard's response, **"DUNAWAY, YOU STAY RIGHT THERE, DON'T MOVE. I AM COMING DOWN TO KISS YOUR A$$."**

It was always fun to be around Howard and his friends, but I was most impressed with him and his mother, Aunt Willie because they were always involved with learning and seemed to know everything. Howard had the correct answers to many of the questions that were posed to contestants on television quiz shows. My aunt took all kinds of courses, and was always embarking on a new project or venture. This made her attractive to both women and men. She was always the center of attention. Unfortunately, Willie died young. She was only in her fifties. Her pallbearers were her current boyfriend and five of her past suitors. What an outstanding lady!

Going to funerals was something I avoided at all costs. I was in my early thirties when Willie died, and when I knew her death was near, I tried to come up with all kinds of excuses to get out of attending her funeral, but could not come up with any I thought my family would accept. Not being able to get out of attending the funeral, I went along with other family members. I learned something profound while listening to my aunt being eulogized—words from friends, church members, and family. I learned about her good works for her neighbors, the time she spent mentoring young people, and her involvement in her church. But most importantly, I had an epiphany, that death was the opposite of life. Just like joy was the opposite of sorrow, or success the opposite of failure, I knew at that moment if I lived long enough many people that I loved would die, and death was a part of life. It was here that I came to terms with my own death, and lost my fear of it.

What I learned? When you embrace your fears, they lose their power.

Chapter
Twelve

We LIVED IN A large three-story, five-bedroom brownstone and my parents rented rooms to out-of-town college students during the summer. They were mostly relatives of my parent's friends. Nathaniel Hunter was an out-of-town student who stayed with us for three consecutive summers. Nathaniel saw it as his personal responsibility to make me smarter, and an overall better person. He was bent on furthering my education, my intellectual and character development. I was 16 and loved the attention that this 19 to 22-year-old, handsome male was paying me. I was an eager student most of the time. When I fell short of completing a work assignment he had assigned me, he would take drastic action, sometimes by twisting my arm. Looking back, I now know he was a bit nuts.

One assignment he gave me was to memorize the poem, "If—" by Rudyard Kipling. The poem is about character and a boy becoming a man. The theme struck a chord in me and although it contains many lovely and important passages, the one that stood out for me was: "If you can talk with crowds and keep your virtue, or walk with kings—nor lose the common touch, If neither foes nor loving friends can hurt you, If all men count with you, but none too much." I have tried to abide by this passage all my life. To me it speaks of humility and the courage and confidence to always be true to you.

The poem is quite long, and I had to learn a new passage every day. If I hadn't memorized the passage when Nathaniel asked me to recite it,

I paid a price. Sometimes the price was to do the dinner dishes. Other times, I had to fold the laundry or some other chore. My mother loved his influence on me, at least at first.

But she was none too happy when she learned that Nathaniel and his friends had taken me to a nightclub. She discovered a picture of us taken at the club with a vodka tonic on the table in front of me. She went on about this for days. I secretly enjoyed all the fuss. But the big blow-up came later and it was one of the worst things I have ever done while playing a joke on someone.

Nathaniel came in one afternoon when a girlfriend of mine was visiting. He invited us up to his room on the third floor to show us something he had purchased. My mother's older sister, Alberta and her boyfriend were visiting from New York, and her boyfriend was sleeping in the bedroom next to Nathaniel's. When we passed that room, the door was slightly ajar. Nathaniel asked, "Who is that jerk sleeping in that room?". "That's my aunts boyfriend from New York." I answered. "Well let's teach that Negro a lesson." Responded Nathanial. When we entered Nathaniel's room, he went in his closet and pulled out his hunting rifle, forgetting all about having invited us up to see his new clothes. He took the rifle and pointed it through the slightly opened door. As we pushed more of the gun barrel through the door, the door made a squeaking sound. This woke my aunt's boyfriend. At first, he looked puzzled. He must have thought he was dreaming. But he heard us when we began to laugh. When we saw recognition in his face, we ran back into Nathaniel's room, still laughing hard, and not thinking how frightened my aunt's boyfriend must have been. We heard him running down the stairs yelling for my Aunt Berta. My aunt and mother were in the kitchen. Shaking, he told them that someone upstairs had pointed a gun at him.

My Aunt Alberta said, "You're drunk. No one pointed a gun at you. You had a nightmare."

But he kept insisting until they agreed to come upstairs and see for themselves. When we heard them in the next room, we could not contain ourselves and our hilarity, and we were found out. We might have escaped discovery if not for our howling with laughter. Upon hearing us, my mother insisted we open the door. Here we were: Nathaniel, Kay and me. Culprits discovered still laughing.

But it was no joke to my aunt and her boyfriend, and they could not be consoled or convinced it was all a joke. We were accused of being on drugs, and of being bums, and thugs. Aunt Alberta and her boyfriend rushed to pack their bags, and left immediately.

My mother was extremely upset with the three of us. But I was the only one she could punish, which resulted in my being restricted to the house, and losing phone privileges for a week. Nathaniel felt sorry for me, and responsible for my plight. As a way of showing support, he helped me with my chores and bought me ice cream. But being sorry did not stop him from badgering, drilling and tutoring me at every turn.

He gave me tips on public speaking, how to stand up and own the space, and how not be intimidated by the audience. He continued to let me go with him and his friends when they took their girlfriends on dates, but not to nightclubs. That was one time only. Nathaniel was from South Carolina and came to Philadelphia to work during the summer to earn money for college. During the first summer, he met an attractive girl named Dee. They became an item and continued their relationship over the winter and into the following summer. The third year into their relationship, Dee became pregnant. When Nathaniel learned of her pregnancy, he promised to return to Philadelphia and marry her. She waited for his return, but he never came back, and she never heard from him again, that we knew of. My family was shocked. We all thought Nathaniel was a terrific and honorable man. Later we heard from mutual friends that he had married his college sweetheart back in South Carolina.

What I learned? Men bear considerable watching, and you need to be aware of even the good guys.

Chapter

Thirteen

*I*F ONE WERE TO search, I am sure they would find a study that revealed a connection between having an unhappy, chaotic home life and depression. Maybe. By the time I entered high school, the years of living with Claude and Ella and all their drama had caught up with me. And I suffered my first bout with depression, although I didn't know at the time that that explained my sadness and feeling of hopelessness.

My mother noticed that I had no energy. Not even to fight with her. But she attributed it to my being lazy and not wanting to do anything she asked, like going to the store or helping her with the housework. I found it hard to do even basic things like going to school or doing homework. My depression got so bad that I could not complete assignments during the second half of eleventh grade. As a result I did not go into the twelfth grade with the rest of my class. Then as now, when I am in trouble, someone or something always steps up like a guardian spirit to help me. At the time, the person came in the form of a guidance counselor, Mrs. Stewart.

Mrs. Stewart was aware that my mental condition would prevent me from attending summer school to make up the courses that I failed. To help me, she arranged for me to work in the school office, to earn the extra credit I needed so I could join my class that fall. My depression was severe. No one suggested that medication might help me cope. There were occasions when I was even unable to work in the office. But Mrs.

Stewart covered for me, and I was not penalized for my absences, and with the extra credits, I was promoted to twelfth grade and graduated on schedule my class.

What I learned? There were people who saw something in me worthy of their support. And I began to feel hopeful and to trust the universe.

When you are down and need a helping hand, and a person appears just at the right time to give you what you need, it can have a profound impact on your life. Mrs. Stewart's intervention and the help she gave to get me promoted to 12th grade was life changing for me. This was the first time someone outside of my family had validated my worthiness. This caused a positive reaction in how I felt about myself. Even though I was in a very low place, having a stranger help me in this way was the beginning and foundation of the faith that has sustained me for more than 50 years. That whenever I am in need, something or someone will come to my aid and show me the way out of my predicament.

My home life remained chaotic, but now I had a new confidence, and hope that things would change for the better, and that I would have a good life. This positive feeling of hope and optimism might have led me to make a premature decision to get married while I was still in high school. To be honest, I saw marriage as an opportunity to escape from my depressing home life and my mother. In any case, I was hopeful and expected my marriage to be a happy one. Clearly, my believing that marrying at seventeen would lead to happiness could be attributed to my youth and immaturity.

I met George Pendleton during my senior year in high school. He was the nephew of one of our neighbors. George was good-looking, funny, and had a personality that lit up a room. He was in the United States Air Force, and was my first serious boyfriend. George was 22, and I thought his being an adult would cause him to expect that our relationship would be sexual. This posed a problem for me because I was afraid that if I had sex, I might get pregnant. This was a very different time. To get pregnant and not be married had a great deal of shame attached to it. My solution to this dilemma was to preempt this possibility by marrying him. I was seventeen, had not graduated from high school; and had only known him for seven months. Insanity! Because I was under the legal age, my parents had to sign for me to get married.

When we approached them about our plans to marry, my father protested, saying I was too young, and needed to complete high school and college before I got married. George assured my father that I would complete high school, and I assured him that I would complete college. My mother voiced no concerns whatsoever. I think she was relieved that I would no longer be her responsibility.

We got married, celebrated with friends and family, and ran into a brick wall. I was clear about why I married George; to escape from my mother. But I didn't know why he married me. In fact, I never gave it a thought. It wasn't until sometime later that I learned why George married me—he needed to escape from a prior relationship. Not an auspicious beginning, and with this as a base, it is no wonder why our marriage was doomed from the start.

Neither of us knew, or understood what partnering with another person meant. George continued to hang out with his guy friends. I was underage and I could not join them at bars or nightclubs. His leaving me alone to be with his friends caused resentment and frequent arguments between us that never got resolved. He thought I was being unreasonable, didn't like his friends and wanted to control him. I thought he was self-centered, selfish, and cold. We had no skills to work through our differences. And over time, we became estranged, one blaming the other for our problems. The irony is that I married George to get away from my mother, only to find I had married my mother.

George was critical, self-centered, and he ignored me. He blamed me when things went wrong, and never took responsibility for any of our problems. Nor did he try to look at things from my perspective. He didn't seem to enjoy my company, only the company of his friends, drinking at bars, or visiting with them on college campuses. I was still 17, much younger than his friends, and felt out of place. Like my mother, George was cold and insensitive to my needs or wishes.

I responded to George's cold treatment of me, in the very same way I had to my mother's cold treatment. I closed my heart to him. This all became very stressful when I became pregnant. We tried to put a good face on our unhappiness, but some things are hard to fake. Here is a scenario of George's reactions at a pivotal point in the last stage of my pregnancy and before the delivery of our first child. At around 8am I began experiencing labor pains. I called George at work to come home because I was in labor. I am not a person who gets overly excited when something serious or traumatic is occurring. So when George arrived I was fixing my hair and preparing myself to go to the hospital. I don't know what he expected. But he said to me. "You are not in labor, and you wasted my time calling me at work when I am very busy." He was so convinced that I was not in labor that he refused to take the bag I had packed for the hospital. Our son, George, was to be born at the Navy Hospital in Philadelphia, which was at the opposite end of Philadelphia from where we lived.

By the time we neared the hospital my labor pains had increased in intensity. I yelled at George when he made the wrong turn when entering the hospital grounds.

"You are going the wrong way, I yelled."

"Shut up! You are not going to die!" he yelled back.

I was more stunned than hurt. We arrived at the hospital at 12:30pm. Our son was born at 1:37. George never acknowledged that he was wrong about my being in labor, and that he had to drive back home to fetch my hospital bag. His attitude did not improve after that, either. When we brought our baby came home from the hospital. I got out of the car, and was stopped because all of the neighbors wanted to see the new baby. George went into the house ahead of me. By the time I walked into the house, George was coming back out. I asked him where he was going. He said a friend just called to say that their friend Bailey was home from college, and all the guys were getting together.

"You are leaving us before we even get into the house?" I asked, incredulous.

"Stop complaining," he shot back. "I am only going to see Bailey."

"F--- Bailey," I exclaimed.

George left anyway.

That I was angry didn't matter to George. He wanted to be with his friends, and he did not care that the baby and I had just home from the hospital. This was just one example of his insensitivity, and he showed his disdain for me in many other ways. I think George was narcissistic like my mother, and resented me if the spotlight was on me and not him. He made snide remarks whenever a friend called to ask my advice.

"You think you know everything," he'd mutter. "You are always telling people what to do."

I think he was jealous that I had friends who valued my opinion.

He was full of put-downs—criticism, and blame. And my resentment of him deepened. It was probably mutual. We had no models to show us how to resolve conflict, or how to be good spouses, and for me, how to be a mother. Clearly we were not prepared for marriage, and I was even less prepared for motherhood. Having no innate skills, my kids paid the price.

What I learned? When trying to solve one problem, you can create another.

Chapter

Fourteen

OF COURSE, GETTING MARRIED young and becoming a mother only served to compound my problems, and to deepen my depression. The lack of knowledge about how to construct a happy family unit added to the stress weighing on both of us. By the age of 21 I had two children and was feeling hopeless, sad and depressed. Unhappy, married with two babies, I felt stuck, overburdened and guilty. Many days it was too difficult to even get out of bed. Sometimes I only had the energy to feed and bathe my children. There was no energy left to fix meals or clean the house. George would come home from work and face a house in disarray—no food on the table and clothes unwashed. We argued because he was unsympathetic to my psychological and emotional state, and I was unsympathetic to his.

"You don't love me!" I would yell.

"Yes, I do," he would respond.

"You don't show it," I would retort.

"Yes I do," he would repeat.

"When, do you show me you love me, I would ask?"

His response?

"Every time I start to hit you and don't."

I thought that was very witty answer, especially coming from George.

But our life was no joke. Sadly, I often thought of suicide as a way out, and spent a lot of time thinking of how I might go about doing it.

This was how I spent my day, thinking of how I might kill myself. And in a bizarre way this gave me comfort—knowing if life got too bad, or if my problems too painful, I could end my suffering by killing myself. Depression, accompanied by suicidal thoughts, has been a continuous struggle for me. I always thought suicide was a component of depression until a psychiatrist told me that suicidal thoughts were tied to an insufficient amount of serotonin in the brain, and many people suffer from depression their whole life without having any suicidal thoughts. This was mind opening, but I didn't learn this until decades later.

Chapter

Fifteen

OUR HAPPIEST MOMENTS AS a family came when we traveled. We were fortunate that George's Air Force career provided numerous opportunities for us to live and vacation in many different places. We first moved to Fairbanks, Alaska, where our youngest son Garry, was born. I was very excited when it was time for us to leave for the airport. This was my first major trip away from Philadelphia. It was a long flight, over 3000 miles to Tacoma, Washington, where we spent the night. We flew another 3000 miles the following day, before we reached Fairbanks where George was assigned to Ladd Air Force Base, now Fort Wainwright Army Base.

Arriving in late December, tired and weary, it took us many hours of sleep to recover. When we finally awoke, we found trees, streets, and mountains—all covered in layers of snow. I had never seen anything more beautiful. It was like awakening in a fairyland. Everything was gleaming and glistening from the snow. We were taken by the sight and excited to be on this new adventure. This was decades ago when Alaska was the last frontier. Here we saw huge moose and caribou up close. We were fortunate enough not to have any encounters with bears, but they were not too far away. The closest we came was seeing them roped on back of trucks, after being shot by hunters.

December 21st is the longest night of the year, with more than 23 hours of darkness. We didn't see daylight until mid-April and we were amazed that people went about their normal activities in total darkness. Kids went to school and came home in the dark. Everyone worked, played, and socialized in the dark. It was not only dark, but extremely cold. The temperature hovered around 30 below zero during most of the winter. Occasionally it dipped to 60 below zero, but never stayed at this low temperature very long.

To keep warm everyone, including children, wore fur coats and fur-lined boots to be protected from the severe cold. To prevent frostbite in this extreme environment, sometimes we had to wear facemasks that left only our eyes and noses visible. Cars had to be plugged into electric outlets so the oil would not freeze. These low temperatures were extremely dangerous and you could not stay out long without getting serious frostbite. If you had a car accident during the winter, which I did, you would die from exposure if not rescued quickly. Many bodies were found under the snow after the thaw came in April. I can't remember how many were ruled as homicides or death by misadventure.

Although we didn't take advantage of the various sporting events that living in Alaska afforded, we never tired of being spectators to the awe-inspiring beauty of the mountains, rivers, and national parks. This was a feast for those who loved outdoor activities—hiking, dog racing over the snow, fishing, and hunting. Fairbanks is the farthest northern city in Alaska, and only a few miles from the North Pole. The Arctic Circle is the most northerly circle of latitude on the globe, and in the Arctic region to its north, the sun doesn't set for one whole day during the summer solstice, June 21st. They call it the Land of the Midnight Sun because a baseball game is played at midnight without lights. The winter solstice is on December 21st, the longest night of the year with more than twenty-three hours of darkness.

Alaska is where I learned how to drive a stick-shift Studebaker. To practice, I got up every day and drove around the base. Impressed with myself, I called a girlfriend to tell her that I had driven for hours without stalling, only to discover that I had driven all that time without changing gears. Eventually, I did get my driver's license, and then I had to learn how to handle a car on snow and ice. This was apparently more challenging than I thought, because I had two automobile accidents. First, I hit a car in front of me that had stopped for a red light. I was under the assumption that by the time I got close to them the light would have turned green, and they would drive on. I was correct in the first part of my assumption, but wrong in the second. The light did turn green before I approached the car, but the car didn't move. By the time that I realized this and pressed on my brakes, I was too close and slid into their rear bumper. The car I hit was new, and the driver was very upset, even accusing me of being drunk. When the police came, they told the driver I was not drunk, and that they could tell by the skid marks that I had tried to stop, but couldn't because of the ice. I refrained from sharing why I didn't try to stop. Assumptions are not to be trusted.

My second car accident occurred after I ignored advice not to use the back gate when leaving the military base, because that route was seldom used. If you had an accident you might be out there for several hours before anyone came by to help you. I did not heed this warning. One morning I picked up a friend who was six months pregnant, to visit another friend who lived in town. Exiting the back gate was more convenient, and put us closer to our friend's house, so I took the back gate. We had not gone more than 1000 yards when I lost control of the car and skidded into a ditch. After we crawled out of the ditch. I asked if she was all right.

She answered, "yes." And then fainted.

The warning I had ignored, to not use the back gate, had caught up with me. I then feared my friend and I might freeze to death. Like many foolish people, we survived only because fate happened to be smiling on us. It was only minutes before a fellow traveler appeared in his truck and pulled us out of the ditch. My Studebaker, though old, held up with no damage, and so did my friend. But, I don't think she ever rode with me again.

Living in Alaska provided many firsts for me. It is where I obtained my first job with the Bureau of Land Management. My boss was the head of the bureau, and he was the best boss I would ever have. He was the boss by which I measured all others in my future. His name was Steve DeRosa, and I loved and respected him completely. He was clear about his expectations—what he rewarded, what he punished, what he did and did not accept, and how your work would be measured. He also gave clear, honest, and direct feedback. When I became a manager, I made every attempt to emulate his management style and put what I learned from him into practice.

Alaska was the first place I experienced an earthquake. For those who have never felt an earthquake, they have missed an experience of sheer terror. By the time I was in another earthquake, while visiting San Francisco, it was a bit less terrifying. But the first time, I was disorientated, and had no idea what was happening. My husband and I were living in a tenth-floor studio apartment. We were eating dinner when all of a sudden the furniture slid to the opposite side of the room—kitchen to living room. By the time we got to the door to try to escape, the earthquake was over. On the Richter scale the quake was mild, and caused very little structural damage, but our fear and emotions scored very high. Two years later, the area suffered a major earthquake with considerable loss of life and property damage. We were blessed; by that time we had moved back stateside.

Chapter

Sixteen

$\mathscr{A}$FTER LIVING IN ALASKA for two and a half years, we moved back to the Philadelphia area. It was a hard adjustment moving to a large city with lots of cars, and fast traffic. George purchased a large Oldsmobile. When he came home from the dealership, I insisted on taking the car for a drive. No one considered that I had been driving an old, slow Studebaker for the past two years. So we all packed into the car: George, Garry, George Jr. and my aunt Pearlie. With me as the driver we took a tour around our neighborhood. Not content with this, I drove to Broad Street, one of the larger streets in Philadelphia. The traffic was brisk, and the car was fast, and I was inexperienced with both. Driving too fast, we approached a traffic light that was turning orange. There was one car in front of me, I assumed at the speed we were traveling, the car in front would go through the orange light. It did not. Realizing this fact too late, I ran into the back of the car. A policeman just happened to be standing there. He motioned for both cars to pull over to the curb. I did, and got out of the car hastily. So hastily, in fact, that I inadvertently left the engine in drive. My car promptly hit the car in front of me a second time, this time with me nowhere near the driver's seat.

The policeman came over and said to me. "Come on, fool me, and tell me you have a driver's license." I showed him my driver's license from Alaska. You can imagine his expression in seeing my license was from Alaska. George started to try and explain something to the policemen.

He stopped him, and said, "Don't bother, I have a wife." Sexist. During the ride home with George driving, no one said a word. They were probably in shock. Although, thankfully, no one was hurt. Unless you count my pride.

During our time in Philadelphia, my son, George, started first grade. I remember him coming home after his first day at school and yelling to kids who were playing outside to be quiet because he was doing his homework. He was in kindergarten. George always had a flair for the dramatic. Not surprisingly, he is now an actor.

Our families were delighted to see us, and we spent many hours talking and sharing family news. Not much had changed—my mother was still drinking, and my parents were still fighting. My kids and I stayed with them while my husband, George, established himself at his new assignment at Dover Air Force Base, in Delaware, Maryland. Our time living in Philadelphia was cut short because of something bad that happened to me.

It was Saturday and George called to say he was not coming home that weekend; he was staying on the military base. This upset me because I had long suspected that he was having an affair, and that *that* was the reason he was not coming home for the weekend. A girlfriend of mine called and invited me to a party that evening. She was a nurse and lived in a high-rise apartment building with her husband, who was also in the Air Force. We were all friends and often partied together. The building's tenants were mostly Air Force medical personnel and someone was always having a party. I told her that George was not coming home that weekend, but she told me to come anyway.

Even though I was feeling a bit blue, I agreed to go. I dressed and arrived at the party around 9 p.m. I knew the two nurses who were hosting the party so I felt welcomed. The place was full of young, attractive, medical people—nurses, interns, and doctors. The crowd was made up of couples and people on their own like me. One guy in particular who was at the party alone asked me to dance several times.

After a few dances, all of a sudden I felt dizzy, and had trouble standing. This had never happened to me before. I thought I was just drunk, but I had had very little to drink. My friends thought I was drunk too, and took me into one of the bedrooms to lie down. The friend who had invited me said I was still asleep when she and her husband got ready to leave. One of the hosts said to let me stay and sleep it off.

Sometime during the night, I awoke and found the guy who had danced with me on top of me. But I couldn't do anything because I blacked out again. When I woke up the next morning there was evidence that I had been raped. After taking a shower and getting dressed, I went up to my friend's apartment and told her what had happened. I still wasn't clear about what had caused me to get dizzy and black out, until she told me that I had probably been drugged. Most of the men at the party were doctors, interns, or medical types, and they all had easy access to drugs and could have easily put something in my drink. She felt bad and responsible because she had left me there, thinking I would be safe. Who wouldn't?

It was very difficult for me to tell George what happened because I knew he would blame me. Which is exactly what happened. He was upset and angry and blamed me for going to the party alone. I didn't take his accusations to heart, since he could have come home and accompanied me to the party, and none of this would have happened. He thought the entire incident was my fault—in a way, I did too. It took a long time to put all of this behind us.

I was able to identify the guy. George found him, and there was a big altercation. George reported him to his commanding officer, but I am not sure if anything was ever done. Decades ago, women were held responsible if they were raped by someone they knew. Shortly after this happened, George was transferred to an Air Force base near London, England.

What I learned? Men bear considerable watching. Some are hunters and some are predators. Women must always be alert when in the company of men.

Chapter

Seventeen

$\mathcal{M}$OVING TO ENGLAND WAS my first experience living outside of the United States. The day we left for England, George and I had a big fight, and I threatened not to go. This did not portend well for our move, or our future relationship. Our flight was Sunday evening at 8:00pm. George left with his uncle Saturday morning to get a haircut, a pretense to get out of the house so he could go say goodbye to his girlfriend. His uncle was his plant and they didn't return until Sunday afternoon. George must have felt some guilt when he came into the house, and all of our friends and relatives were there to say goodbye. As he entered the house, he greeted everyone with a single hello. He didn't act like someone who have been gone for over twenty-four hours after saying he was only going to get a haircut. His barber must have been in New York.

When I asked where he had been his response was, "None of your damn business."

I responded in kind, calling him some choice words. I said I was not moving to England with him. He probably didn't care. But my relatives and friends persuaded me to go, encouraging me and saying that things would work out. My girlfriend's mother, Mrs. Bell, was a bit more understanding. She said, "honey just do the best you can." I didn't need much persuading, I was excited to be moving to London.

We flew out of an Air Force base in New Jersey on Sunday evening, and arrived in England 8am the following morning. The sky was overcast, and everything looked grey and dull. We were all jet-lagged and slept the entire first day, but were up bright and early the second morning eager to see our new world. It was a cold December day, and we wrapped up in our warm coats and off we went to see the sights. Our first surprise came as a shock. We stopped at a vendor and bought hotdogs. As was our custom we loved our hotdogs with plenty of mustard. So we piled it on. After taking a bite, neither of us could breathe. We experienced a piercing pain through our noses and at the top of our heads. We didn't finish our hotdogs, and never used English mustard again.

After spending 30 days in a bed and breakfast, we moved into a lovely three-bedroom Tudor home on Cunningham Park, and got George and Garry into school. We enrolled George in the American School on the military base. Garry was too young for first grade, so we enrolled him in an English school where he became a proper English lad—short pants and a British accent. Our house in Cunningham Park, Harrow On the Hill, was famous for the Harrow prep school in the area. I think Winston Churchill attended school there. Our boys adjusted well, and quickly, made friends with their English neighbors.

Soon we were off busy exploring our new surroundings. Visiting places and enjoying the famous landmarks of London—Buckingham Palace, the Houses of Parliament, and Tower of London. Every weekend we went sightseeing and enmeshed ourselves in the many sights and sounds of our new home.

England, being an English-speaking country, made the transition to a foreign land easy and comfortable. However, there were challenges— driving on the opposite side of the road, maneuvering around the roundabouts, turning left from the right lane while shifting gears, and pressing the clutch. Taking to the road was a chilling and daring undertaking.

One day while driving with my sons to go shopping, I misjudged the distance between two trucks and ended up smashed between them. I slid out of the driver's side, with glass covering my face. My sons managed to stay in the car; fortunately they weren't injured. People stopped to offer assistance. One woman recognized me from the women's club.

"Mrs. Pendleton," she said. "Are you all right?"

I could not answer for fear of getting glass in my mouth. When the ambulance came, they put me on a stretcher and placed me in the ambulance, but neglected to strap me in. Thank God I was conscious because I had to hold on for dear life as they traversed the roundabouts at sixty or more kilometers per hour. With my children inside the car, the police followed the ambulance to the hospital. Having escaped being thrown from the stretcher, I ended up with only a mild concussion as a result of my head being struck during the collision. All things considered, I was lucky and soon fully recovered. Although they weren't hurt, my sons refused to ride with me for a long time. My reputation for being an at-risk driver has followed me to this day.

But nothing overshadowed our excitement and joy as we toured and spent time getting to know this new world. There was always a new attraction or famous place to visit—Madame Tussaud's, Westminster Abbey, the Houses of Parliament, Stratford-upon-Avon (where William Shakespeare was born and buried), and Blenheim Palace (birthplace of Winston Churchill, who guided Britain and the allies through the crisis of World War II). We took trips through the beautiful countryside and joined the crowds in Piccadilly Circus in the West End of London, which housed numerous theatres. Piccadilly Circus is close to major shopping and entertainment areas and attracts loads of tourists from around the world and is noted for its neon signs. We totally immersed ourselves in the novelty and richness of this vibrant city and country.

George and I struggled on as a couple. Although he was not happy with me, he was a very attentive and a loving father to our children. In the early years, it was George who they most relied on. Who went to them when they were having a nightmare? George. It was George who went to all of their Little League games, and who took them with him to all of his afternoon sports events. They were his buddies, and he enjoyed being with them. They had a dad who was a lot of fun, and who even their friends loved to be with. Our sons and their friends enjoyed spending time with him all of his life. Unlike George, I didn't have any kid in me and didn't know how to entertain and have fun with little people. I still don't. It wasn't until years later that I learned about good mothering, and how children needed to be hugged, nurtured, and given emotional support. These are things you should learn from mirroring your relationship with your mother. Unfortunately, my mother had not learned them either.

At that time, my idea of good mothering was to prepare my children for life—doing things with them that would make them smart. I spent my time teaching them how to play chess, how to read and understand what was written in the newspaper and how to appreciate art. By the age of four, they could play chess well. George, Jr. could beat many of our friends. I was worried once when he didn't come home after dark. When he finally arrived an hour later, I asked him why he was late. He said he had been playing chess with our neighbor, Mr. Hogan, and Mr. Hogan, would not let him leave until he had won a game. George was only seven.

I read to my sons and discussed what was in the news. Whether it was politics, the stock market, history, Black history, or art history—we talked about it. When they were much older, George told me he and Garry wanted to go out and play instead of conversing about who might have painted Van Gogh's "Wheat Fields" or Rembrandt's "The Night Watchman." We both laughed.

What I am about to write might sound crazy, but my behavior with my children derived from a deep fear that I might die while they were still young, and I wanted to prepare them to think, to have their own opinions, to judge things for themselves, and have the courage to stand up for themselves. I thought knowledge was power, and that it was my personal power that helped me through my sad and difficult childhood. But I now know that my behavior was also based on my fear, that if I loved them too much they might die, and I would not be able to cope with the pain. This was the same coping skill I used when I closed my heart, and stopped loving my parents when I was eight or nine years old.

Don't feel.

What I learned? You can't give what you don't have, and you raise your children in response to your own childhood—whether good or ill.

Chapter

Eighteen

*L*IVING IN ENGLAND PROVIDED many new and novel opportunities for us. I went to work for the United States Navy, enrolled at the University of Maryland (London Campus), and made television commercials for Carling's Black Label beer. Sometimes I felt like a movie star. Once, when I didn't show up for a taping session because I didn't have our car, they sent a driver for me. We actors were paid well for every ad we made, but we had to a sign a form that we would not be paid residuals. I only saw one of the ads I made after returning to the United States—it was of me on the big red English bus.

Both my sons, George and Garry, were featured on television shows. Garry was a participant on the Art Linkletter show, *Kids Say the Darndest Things*, in England. He was one of four six-year-olds on the show. They all gave hilarious answers when Art Linkletter asked how their parents met or other questions that provoked embarrassing or funny responses from the kids.

George was green with envy when Garry received a large box of toys as a gift for being on the show. But his time came a few months later when he was chosen to be on the BBC television show American *Kids Living In England."* The other four American kids on the show gave very negative answers when asked what they liked about living in England. They probably just repeated what they had overheard their parents say. George, on the other hand, was positive and was a big hit because he knew the names of the British football players who had just won the FIFA World Cup.

The following Saturday after George's television interview, my husband and I attended a black tie event at a London hotel. The guests were a mixture of English and Americans. During the reception, we met a lovely English woman. Upon learning we were American, she told us that she had seen the cutest little Black American boy on a BBC television show, who knew so much about English football. She was astonished when I told her that the cute little Black American boy was my son George. She ran off to find her husband and brought him back to meet us and introduced us to their other friends. George made us famous for a night.

The times that we spent at the base club were fun times too. The four of us would have dinner and then go into the ballroom and dance to the latest songs by the Beatles' or other English bands. One particular song by the Beatles' that we loved was "Hey Jude." When we were not trying to learn a new American dance, we participated in and danced with the English. "The Hokie Pokey" was our favorite. You put your right foot in, your left foot out…and you shake it all about. Or something similar to this. We all loved to dance and we were all good dancers.

It seemed in England everything was good, new and exciting. We were fortunate that we were able to travel and vacation in many of the major cities in Europe. These experiences were life changing on many levels—educational, cultural, intellectual, and psychological. Traveling and meeting people from different countries gave us a sense of being a part of a larger world. It gave us enormous confidence that allowed us to be at home everywhere and to accept novelties with comfort and ease.

I augmented this educational windfall with my own pursuit of a formal education. At first, George did not support me in this endeavor.

He said it was okay for me to attend college as long as it did not interfere with my wifely duties. I cannot write here my response to this statement, but it was a strong one. I enrolled in school and continued my studies while living in England. Then I transferred to the University of Maryland, College Park when we moved to Washington, D.C.

Chapter

Nineteen

*T*HE JOYFUL MEMORIES OF our four years in England stayed with us. We relived the trips we took and the excitement and fun we had while driving to foreign places, and singing songs by the Beatles – *She Loves you, yeah, yeah, yeah, … with a love like that you know you must be glad.* These were our best times, and we had a special remembrance for every place we visited, each held its own magic and wonder. Cities like Cologne, Munich, Vienna, Paris, Rome, Venice, and Barcelona were all unique and different. But none of these places could match the exhilaration I felt while living and working in Washington, D.C.

Before moving to D.C., I was a political novice with no political leanings that I could intelligently support. It was D.C. where I got my first exposure to national politics and I loved it. Being immersed in our national history, and flooded daily with the most pressing and interesting political news provided the spark for my political interest.

George, the boys, and I explored the city, visiting the historic monuments of George Washington, Abraham Lincoln, and Thomas Jefferson. We continued by visiting the national buildings and institutions—the White House, The Capitol, and the Supreme Court. We steeped ourselves into our nation's history, and experienced the joy and pride of being Americans.

This pride was buffeted when I accepted a job at what was then named the Budget Bureau. The Budget Bureau was part of the executive offices of the president, and it was housed in the ornate and historic executive office building that was full of charm and character.

To work at the Bureau you needed a top-secret security clearance. Some of my Philadelphia, evil-thinking friends thought this might be a good opportunity to get back at me by lying to the FBI about my character when they were interviewed. But, my friends must have said I was of good character because I received the top-secret security clearance and was hired by the Bureau. It was thrilling to be working in the executive offices of the president and it was a joy to drive to work every day into this exciting and beautiful city from where I lived in Maryland. Very heady stuff for a young woman from Philadelphia.

Bureau employees were invited to attend ceremonies at the White House. My first time seeing President and Mrs. Lyndon Johnson was when they hosted some foreign dignitaries in the Rose Garden. There were many other opportunities to be present at ceremonies under the Johnson Administration and during the Nixon years. We attended numerous speeches in the East Room of the White House. At that time, we were allowed to take videos and pictures, and I still have some home movies of the presidents and their families.

It was during the Vietnam War when the "Stop the War Movement" was at its height, that I resigned from the Bureau and enrolled at the University of Maryland. Students against the war took over the building my first day of classes. Although I shared their sentiments, I was very scared. We were literally on lockdown. Similar incidents were happening all over the entire country. Eventually, the anti-war demonstrators were successful in forcing President Johnson to give up on the chance to seek reelection. The war continued under President Nixon for many more years, as the anti-war protests increased in intensity.

And there I was learning about politics and political parties firsthand. I examined where I stood on issues, in general, and on the war in particular. Reading the *Washington Post* every day, gave me a great political education. It helped me to access and understand the different political parties and their platforms. I choose to be a part of the Democratic Party for several reasons. First, I am a Black female, and the Democratic Party was the one that most supported equal rights and equal opportunities for women and people of color. Second, Democrats support unions that are needed to protect workers' rights. Third, Democrats supported and still support social security. Fourth, they best support the middle-class, and protect the vulnerable and the powerless.

Living and working in this highly charged political climate was how I was exposed to different political parties, politicians, and platforms. After analyzing and sifting through all the political rhetoric, my views evolved and created the foundation for my activism. I have fond memories of those times, and the excitement I felt when I attended receptions or events in the White House. The euphoria is still there whenever I fly to Washington D.C. and the nation's capital comes into view. The city is beautiful and historic. Many years later, to my amazement, I attended President Barack Obama's first inauguration—THE NATION'S FIRST BLACK PRESIDENT. I was so proud. My sister-in-law said her son Brian was so high he didn't need a plane to bring him back to Boston. Statistics stated that there were four to five million people in the city and the police did not make one arrest—it was magical. It was clearly one of the highlights of my life.

What I learned? For every time there is a season. And the majesty and grandeur of political power allows the powerful elite to rule like czars.

Chapter

Twenty

BEFORE WE MOVED FROM the Washington area, we had a frightful experience. Our son Garry was missing. This was one of my greatest fears. That something would happen to my children. It was after dark one evening. Both boys had been told to come home before dark. George came in, and we asked where his brother was. He said he didn't know. He had not seen him. Garry was only eight years old, and after contacting our neighbors, no one knew where he was, or might be. We were living in the suburbs of Maryland, near Washington, D. C. Finally, someone told us that they saw Garry riding his bike. He had always obeyed us, when we told him to be home before dark. It had been dark now for a few of hours, and we really began to worry, especially when it started raining very hard. His dad drove around the neighborhood looking for him, but came up empty handed. Now our worry turned into panic.

Around nine o'clock our phone rang. The caller asked to speak to Mrs. Pendleton. I said, "I am Mrs. Pendleton." She said, "I am Mrs. Austin, and I have your son Garry." I have never felt such joy and relief in my life. She said, "Don't worry, I have dried him off and gave him some hot soup." After George picked him up, we asked him what had happened to him. He told us he was riding his bike and was deliberately trying to get lost. He thought if he rode far away from our area, he would be able to use the neon lights from the supermarket to guide him back home.

What he didn't count on was it being a Sunday, when the supermarket closed early.

I asked him how he came to be in the company of Mrs. Austin. He explained that after he got lost and it started to rain, he knocked on her door and told her he was lost.

I asked, "Why that door?" "Why did you chose to knock on that door?"

"Mom, you always told me if I ever got in trouble, to go to the house where the blinds are open because you thought people with open blinds would be more open to helping me."

What I learned? Your children listen to you even when you think they don't. So keep telling them what you want them to know.

Chapter
Twenty-One

$\mathcal{W}$E ALL FELT A sense of loss when we had to move away from Washington, D. C. We had grown to love and appreciate this wonderful city, but George had been transferred to an Air Force base in Oklahoma City. Separating from all of our friends and activities was difficult. There was quite a contrast between living in Washington, D.C. and living in Oklahoma City, but we made the best of it, and quickly adjusted to living in the Midwest and found a lot there to appreciate.

One of my first actions was to transfer from the University of Maryland to the University of Oklahoma and continue my education. I soon discovered that in the mid-west, college football is king. The rivalries between the Universities of Oklahoma, Nebraska and Texas were legendary. As if to exemplify how important these games were, the president of our university told us if we beat the University of Texas at Saturday's game, he would cancel school on Monday. I was dumbfounded. The notice was published, distributed, we won the game, and Monday's classes were dutifully cancelled.

It was great not having to attend classes on Monday, but coming from the East Coast where professional football was revered, it was like a cultural shock, and took some getting used to. The year we moved to Oklahoma, Oklahoma and Nebraska were vying to be the number one college team in the nation. The week before the big game the entire state was electrified, and people were in a frenzy with anticipation, everyone shouting, "We are number one!"

Both the Speaker of the House, who was from Oklahoma, and the governor of our state attended the pep rallies. They called it the "game of the century" and played it on Thanksgiving Day. Sadly, Oklahoma lost the game.

We were a football family—our sons played Pop Warner football, my husband had played semi-pro ball, and was our kid's football coach. So we were ardent fans of the University of Oklahoma, and very vested in their winning the game. After the game, we all had sad faces, disappointed that the University of Oklahoma lost to the University of Nebraska and missed the opportunity to be NUMBER ONE.

We embraced our new home with enthusiasm: sampling the food, touring the City's museums and learning about the area's history. On the weekends we took trips and explored our environment to discover the uniqueness of this new place where we lived. One trip that stands out in my memory is when we attended a sea bass festival on a lake that separated Oklahoma from Texas. Here we listened to country music played on banjos, saw more than thousand people dressed in overalls and straw hats eating fried fish, coleslaw, and hush puppies. What was the greatest puzzle for me was how they kept so much fish fresh so they could feed that amount of people. We all joined right in, singing, eating, and listening to the unfamiliar accent of the people from this area. It was a different culture and we enjoyed it.

Sometimes we traveled with our German shepherd, Gep, which was a bit uncomfortable because he would stand behind me slobbering down my back. Gep was a beautiful dog. His coat was a combination of black and brown. He was very intelligent, and loved to play. Everyone in the neighborhood knew him, he was like the community dog. He often walked the kids to the school bus and to church on Sunday mornings. Many times our phone rang requesting that we come to church and get Gep because he was standing outside the church door and frightening the parishioners who were attending church. He was also a great guard dog. I found out just how great a guard dog he was, and how very intelligent he was. Sometimes George and I arrived home after dark, and Gep would always be sitting guarding the front door when the kids had left it open. On this particular evening we arrived home after dark, and found the front door open, but no Gep there guarding the door. We became alarmed, and entered the house with some trepidation. What we found was Gep guarding the back door, which the kids left open. Gep made the choice to guard the back door instead of the front door to provide what he saw as the greatest protection. This demonstration of our dog's devotion to our family moved us greatly. But Gep's greatest value was opening my closed heart.

Since childhood when I decided to stop loving my parents, unbeknownst to me, I could not feel love for anything. This was the cost of protecting myself from being hurt by my parents. My internal message was not to feel as to avoid getting hurt. This emotional protection came with a price—emotional numbness.

Somehow falling in love with GEP changed all this. The wall around my heart melted. I could feel pain, joy, and sadness. All emotions became available to me.

I had never had a dog before, and didn't know how precious they could be. Nor did I know they possessed personalities, or that there was such depth to their intelligence. Gep had a German Shepard friend, Sparky, who lived up the street. When Gep visited him, Sparky would use his nose to open the gate, and he and Gep would run, play, and have a great time together.

I loved our dog so much and appreciated his gift of unconditional love. Our entire family suffered when we gave him to a loving family when we moved from Oklahoma to Florida because we didn't have accommodations for him there. I still think of him and miss him to this day.

What I learned? Love will open a closed heart.

Chapter
Twenty-Two

GEORGE AND I STRUGGLED on as a couple, but he really enjoyed being a father to our sons, at least at this point. He was a loving and hands on dad. He spent time teaching them how to play sports: football, basketball, and baseball. If he wasn't coaching their team, he was on the sideline cheering them on. Later he involved them in golf. Their relationship was close, and they shared a lot of experiences with his male friends and their sons. George was a man's man. Always quick to laugh, he was a lot of fun to be around and was popular with people of all ages. Our sons and their friends enjoyed spending time with him into his older years.

Later things changed between him and our son, Garry. As our marriage deteriorated, Georges' behavior towards Garry turned aggressive and mean. I always thought George favored our older son George, but it wasn't until later when things between us really crumbled, that he demonstrated that he was partial to George, in the way he treated and reacted to them. He started picking on Garry for any and everything. Garry became the scapegoat for George's unhappiness, like I was for my mother's. George was reluctant to confront me for fear I might leave him. So Garry became the recipient of his displaced anger. And he overreacted to any and every small infraction that Garry committed, like leaving his bike on the ball field, or forgetting his lunch money, or baseball glove. George's actions were as if Garry had stolen something. He was constantly criticizing, blaming, and accusing Garry of God-knows-what. This became a big problem in our marriage, and we fought over his treatment and my protection of Garry, which added to the list of my grievances.

What I learned? In troubled families the weakest person becomes the scapegoat.

Chapter

Twenty-Three

ALTHOUGH MY HEART OPENED, I still did not have the requisite parenting skills that my children needed and still fell short in the parenting department. In many ways I repeated the behavior of my parents. No touching or hugging. Not being involved with their activities, like going to their games, or baking cakes for the cakewalk. I was pretty much a hands-off parent. Only coaching from the sidelines. I am sure this affected my children in ways they don't even know.

My mother and father were not very good parents, and I felt this loss during my childhood into my adulthood. They were what one might refer to as negligent and uninvolved. I was allowed to do almost anything without supervision or being disciplined. On the positive side, the benefit is I am very spontaneous and don't fear what others think of my actions. But this freedom caused me to feel lonely and abandoned as a child, as if my parents didn't care enough to say no. I remember one day when I was around nine or ten years old, I was visiting my two girl cousins near my age. I asked them to go to the corner drugstore to buy ice cream cones—I had the money. They agreed and were very excited.

"Let's go," I said.

"Ok," they said. "But we have to go and ask our mother."

I remember feeling very sad that I didn't have to ask anyone.

It's no surprise that I mirrored my parent's mistakes. Not nurturing, or participating, or joining them in their games. This lack of involvement is reflected in my sons being underachievers. Although they are both very intelligent and talented, they are still searching to find who they should be. I think this is because I spent so much time finding myself rather than giving them what they needed. I feel responsible for their lack of direction and for their not being as successful as their talents would indicate.

I still worry about their futures and who they might be later in their lives, although they are over forty years old. It is in this sense that I am paying now for what I did not provide for them when they were young. On the plus side, both of my sons are spontaneous, independent, and confident. They don't care what others think of them. I hope, like me, they will bloom, and be all they can be.

PART TWO

Chapter

Twenty-Four

BEING A MILITARY FAMILY, we moved every few years. This time we moved from Oklahoma to Florida, leaving the West and going to the South. Living in Florida brought change and opportunity. We lived in a beautiful apartment, on Bayshore Drive on the Tampa Bay. Waking up in the mornings and seeing the water was calming to my spirit. This was a period in my life where I spent a lot of time alone. With my kids in school and my husband working, I had time to ride my bike, take tennis lessons, and play bridge with women who were retired and lived in the area. I asked them what it was like being retired and living in Florida? They said it was depressing. I asked why. Their answer was "everyday there is either an ambulance or a hearse in your block." This told me that I would never retire in Florida.

I had plenty of time for contemplation, and I discovered that I liked myself, and that I enjoyed my own company. Time alone provided an opportunity for me to get to know myself, and served to erase some of the negative impact to my self-esteem that was fostered by my mother.

My self-esteem continued to improve as I encountered people who liked me and gave me positive feedback. After spending several months enjoying my own company, I took a job with the Veterans Administration, providing administrative support to three psychologists who also taught at the University of Tampa. All three of my bosses took a personal interest in me.

One said, "Claudette, you are undereducated for your intelligence." "Claudette can figure people out better than anyone I have ever known," said another.

"Claudette, your comments and feedback enhance my thoughts and my writing," the third one told me.

Working with them boosted my confidence and my interest in psychology, which is the field in which I later received both undergraduate and graduate degrees.

Our time living in Tampa was shortened when George left the Air Force and accepted a position as a computer engineer with Digital Equipment Corporation in the Boston area. My plan was to complete my college degree in Boston. But I got waylaid when I met a human resource representative who invited me to interview for a position at Digital Equipment Corporation. I was offered the position and I accepted.

My first professional job at Digital was as an equal employment opportunity representative. My responsibilities were to execute the company's plan to hire and promote more women and minorities to management positions. We developed a training program and educated managers about the benefits of the company's affirmative action program, and encouraged them to work with their senior staff in the recruitment, interviewing and selection process. Before we could implement the program, an internal audit was required.

The purpose of the audit was to reveal disparities in the company's recruiting, hiring, and promoting of women and minorities processes. I volunteered to design and conduct the audit for the administration and finance organizations. My team and I reviewed the company's human resource records on how women and minorities fared in hiring, promotions, and discipline, as compared to White males, and wrote a report on any discrepancies that we found.

The results of the audit were not surprising—they revealed that compared to White males, women and minorities were grossly underrepresented in all areas. When management received and reviewed the report, they committed to taking corrective action. At that time, Digital was seen as a progressive and positive place for women and minorities to work, and most departments increased their numbers of both groups.

Designing and conducting the first audit in the company increased my visibility and helped advance my career. I got promoted and served in various management roles— organization development, employee relations, recruitment and placement, and human resource and training. Performing in these roles and participating on management teams gave me a first-hand view of corporate politics, power, and the unwritten rules. Some I have included in this book as a way of helping women navigate what were pitfalls for me in my young professional career.

What I learned? Corporate Success is based on the ability to recognize, acquire, and use power.

Chapter
Twenty-Five

$\mathscr{A}$S MY CAREER PROGRESSED, my marriage floundered. Both George and I were unhappy, but I was the one who complained. Not wanting to give up and still trying to save our marriage, I made an appointment for us to see a marriage counselor. George agreed to go, but with the attitude that I was the problem and that the counselor should work on fixing me. To some extent this was true. I was the one who acted out by yelling and screaming at him when he blamed me for everything, and took no responsibility when things went wrong. It was difficult for me to complain about George to my friends and relatives because they could see no fault in him. This was because he never took a stand, and was always charming and agreeable, at least on the surface.

My bosses always enjoyed meeting and talking with him, and thought he was the best.

All of my friends, relatives, and even strangers loved George. They all thought he was wonderful. People would often come up to me when we were on vacation and say, "Your husband is a great guy!"

I would say to George, "How does the world love you, and I hate you?"

I carried a lot of guilt hating this "wonderful guy." It was confusing because he didn't do things that I could identify and point to. He always seemed to go along with whatever I wanted, a good guy. I often felt misunderstood and underappreciated by people because this is what they saw. They didn't see it was me telling George to call them on their birthday, or send to flowers, or to stop by and say hello when he was in their town. I was the sensitive one, but they saw me as the bad person because I always spoke my mind.

George was passive-aggressive, but I didn't know it at the time and his behavior made me crazy.

For example, I told him once that we never spend any time together.

"I go to school all week," I said. "And you play golf on Saturday, go to the club, and play cards all day Sunday. Next Sunday I will go with you to the club and have breakfast."

"Okay," he said.

The next Sunday we went to the club. George took me to the dining room and said he was going to the stag bar, and would be right back. After waiting for him for twenty minutes, I went to the stag bar to find him. (Women were not allowed into the stag bar at that time.) I stood at the door until I caught George's eye; he indicated that he would be right out. I went back to the dining room and waited another fifteen minutes. When he didn't come, I became enraged. I was ready for battle. When I went back to the stag bar, I was restrained from entering by the doorman, and this made me even angrier. So I yelled at the top of my voice.

"GEOOORGE!"

He ran out the door pass me into the parking lot. When I caught up with him, I asked him a question.

"Why didn't you come to the dining room so we could have breakfast, I waited over 30 minutes for you?"

"I already ate breakfast in the stag bar," George answered." Why do you think I came here with you, I asked? You said you wanted to come and have breakfast, you didn't say you wanted to come here and have breakfast with *me*. So I brought you. You didn't say you wanted to eat *with me*."

Now really, he couldn't be that dumb, could he?

Here lies the rub. Whenever I attempted to discuss our relationship and what made me unhappy, he would say, "Why do you always want to start something?" Even when I tried to initiate sex, it turned into something I was attempting to do against him. Sunday was my day of leisure. It was also the day of the football games. If I tried to get romantic, he accused me of trying to interfere with his watching the game. Sometimes when he wanted to go to the club to watch the game or to see his friends, he would deliberately provoke me to start a fight so he could use it as a ruse to leave the house, sometimes for days. It was not until years later after we divorced that he confessed to provoking the fights so he could leave the house.

When I shared this with a female friend, she said, "I don't care how much I yell at my husband, he had better not leave even for one day."

What I learned? When you are young and inexperienced, you are easily manipulated and men bear considerable watching.

Chapter

Twenty-Six

𝓕ORTUNATELY, THE MARRIAGE COUNSELOR was not able to fix me, nor improve our relationship. We hung on for three years longer because I was reluctant to end the marriage and hurt our children. After years of marriage, I also felt some responsibility for George, who said he was unhappy but didn't want to leave me. When I shared this with the therapist—that both George and I were unhappy, but George did not want a divorce and I felt guilty about leaving him—the therapist said, "Maybe George did not expect to be happy, but you did. And if you leave George and he sits in the corner with a thumb in his mouth for the rest of his life that is on George, and not on you."

This statement lifted a weight I had been carrying for a long time. I wanted to leave George but was held back because he didn't want me to leave him, even though he would not do anything to improve the marriage. I had also bought into the adage that you can't build your happiness on someone else's unhappiness. The therapist's statement was liberating, and helped me to let go of the guilt, and to feel that I could leave George and do what was best for me. But still, I stayed.

The final push, or tipping point came when I read a book that introduced me to the concept of "the intimate enemy." The definition of an intimate enemy is someone who is close to you and professes to care about you, but constantly undermines and thwarts your efforts. They can be a sibling, parent, spouse, or best friend. The way to recognize an intimate enemy is to examine their behavior in response to you. Do they try to sabotage your goals or put you down? If you are on a diet, do they bring you candy? If you have a win, do they criticize you instead of cheering you`? When something they do goes wrong do they blame you? If you get a promotion, do they say you are just lucky?

Most importantly, when you are in the presence of an intimate enemy, you feel dejected. As I read through the list describing this behavior, I knew immediately that I was married to an intimate enemy. Of the fifteen examples given, George met twelve of them. I remember calling him a bunch of names because, up until that point, I had accepted all the blame for the trouble in our marriage. This information opened my eyes and reduced the guilt I was feeling about wanting a divorce.

I no longer felt responsible for our dysfunctional relationship, but I still did not leave because I lacked the courage to go out on my own. I moved from my parent's house to my husband's house when I got married, and I had never lived alone. The very thought of it caused me intense anxiety until a friend explained why he thought this was a problem. His explanation was that I had been left alone too early as a small child. He said children build up confidence to be alone gradually. The small child becomes anxious when the mother leaves his sight, but feels reassured when he sees her come out from behind a door, or reappears. The reassurances are accumulated, as the child grows older and more confident. He can be on his own with his mother in the next room, then she can go up the stairs, then leave him alone for longer periods without him suffering anxiety. My friend told me that I had been left alone too early without my mother appearing again to reassure me.

This explanation made sense and it reduced my anxiety about living alone.

What I learned? The teacher will appear when the student is ready to learn.

Chapter
Twenty-Seven

$\mathcal{M}$Y COURAGE WAS FURTHER bolstered when I read an article in the *Boston Globe* Sunday paper. It featured a story about a warlock (a male witch). If I remember correctly, his name was Ted and he lived in Westborough, MA. According to the article, Dartmouth College had researched his predictions and reported that more than seventy percent of them had come true.

I took this as a sign, and was very excited because my secretary Sharon lived in Westborough and I convinced her to accompany me on my search to locate this warlock. I needed confirmation that I had made the right decision to get divorced.

Sharon and I took off during lunch, and after getting directions from several people we finally found Ted's house. We knocked on the door and a man with a ghostly complexion, and white hair, dressed in a black robe, opened the door and greeted us. I quickly explained that I had read about him in the *Boston Globe* and wanted to meet with him to get a reading. He gave me an appointment for the next day. I was a bit anxious about keeping the appointment and insisted that my Sharon go with me. I wanted support and I wanted a witness to his predictions.

I had no idea of what the home of a warlock would look like. What we found was a house that was old and dark, with stuffed animal heads on the walls. It was more than a bit creepy. He asked me why I came and what I wanted from the session. I told him that I wanted to get divorced, but was frightened that I might be making the wrong decision. He asked me to give him something I was wearing. I gave him my wedding ring. He turned it over several times before beginning his predictions. Here's what he told me:

- Get a divorce
- It is not a terrible marriage, but it is not your cup of tea
- Many people will tell you not to get a divorce, but do not listen to them
- You are going to have a fabulous new life
- You are going to be returning to school
- You should never swim in the ocean, it would not be safe, only swim in swimming pools
- Nothing will ever happen to you while flying
- You have been thinking of getting involved with someone, but it had not happened and it would be short lived
- You should be very careful because I saw your boots on ice
- You are going to meet a White man in the fall; on the surface you seem very different, but you will be like two peas in a pod
- You are going to move and live in a foreign country
- Do not be afraid to get a divorce because you are going to have a fantastic new life

I wrote everything down, and told my friends because I wanted witnesses who could confirm whether his predictions came true or not.

Eighteen months after my secretary and I met with Ted the warlock, she got married and my escort to her wedding was the White man that the warlock predicted I would meet.

If Ted was a charlatan, I can't say. I can only attest that after more than thirty years, most of his predictions have come true:

- I divorced
- I returned to school and received a master's degree
- I got involved with someone in a relationship that was short lived
- The White man contacted me in the fall and we have been happily married for over thirty years
- I have moved and worked in a foreign country
- I have had a fantastic life

The warlock encouraged me to make the decision I wanted to make and his prediction that I would have a fantastic life is still coming true.

What I learned? Angels appear in different forms to guide you; you just need to recognize them and follow their lead.

Chapter

Twenty-Eight

$\mathcal{W}$ITH SOME FEAR AND trepidation I started the process of leaving George. I left my sons with George because I wanted to be free of responsibility for the first time in my adult life. I also thought that since they were boys, they would be better off with their father. He was also a better parent.

Even though I wanted the divorce, I found it emotionally draining. I thought this is so hard, how can so many people do it? My friend told me that when it is more painful to stay, than to leave, is when people get divorced. It was years before I lost the pull to go back to George and make our family hold again. And I forever missed the part that was good about us. When I shared my thoughts on this with my psychology professor, this was his explanation—When something is bad, it is seldom completely bad. When we separate from the bad or the minus, we still miss what was good or the positive.

Wanting some physical distance between George and me, I requested to be transferred to a Digital facility in Springfield, MA, which was 90 miles from our corporate office in Maynard, MA. Springfield was close enough that I could return and spend the weekend with my sons, George and Garry. I remember reading somewhere that most people are naturally afraid when embarking on a new course into the unknown. This was true of me when I transferred to the new position of buyer, where previously I have been in human resources, and moved to a new town.

My new job was purchasing electronic components in the Digital Springfield plant. This was the loneliest, saddest, and most boring time of my life. Springfield was not a good place to be single. Sometimes I was so lonely my face ached. I found solace in reading poetry. There was one particular poem that brought me comfort, and I read it every night. It was titled, "Waiting", by John Burroughs. The essence of the poem was not to be sad, or impatient, but to have faith and hope because the person you are seeking, is also seeking you.

What I learned? Stay strong and keep faith when you're down that there will be a better tomorrow.

Chapter
Twenty-Nine

GEORGE AND I DIVORCED, but kept in close proximity because of our boys. Some years later, when we were talking, he said to me, "We never had a chance." He was referring to our families of origin. We both came from similar circumstances; violent, chaotic and unhappy homes. My mother was an alcoholic and so was George's father. My mother treated me harshly and took her anger out on me. George's dad chased him out of the house with a baseball bat when he was drunk and angry. George said this happened often. He would be asleep and would be awakened by his father cursing him, and his mother, yelling, "Run, Junie! Run!"

I am sure our family's drama somehow connected and drew us together. Someone once said, "Marriages are not made in heaven, they are made in the subconscious."

After our separation, I was able to accept that neither of us was to blame for our failed marriage. George and I remained emotionally close until his death from colon cancer. He and his wife had moved to Colorado with their twin daughters. And our sons went there and cared for him the last two months of his life. Just as when George was a young man, everyone still loved him. As evidence, he had three memorial services—one in Boulder, Colorado where he died, one in suburban Philadelphia where he was born, and one in Nashua, New Hampshire where he lived for many years after our divorce. A few weeks before his death I called his home to speak to my son Garry to ask how his dad was doing. His father heard him on the phone and asked whom he was talking to.

"Mom," Garry answered.

He wanted to speak with me. He told me he thought he would be all right and I told him I agreed with him, that he would be all right. I, then, asked him if I had ever thanked him for getting me out of Philadelphia. He laughed.

I said, "I love you."

He said, "I love you very much."

It was a beautiful ending for us.

What I learned? The longer I live and the people I care for die, the more I miss them. They leave an empty place in my heart. I think this might be the result of closing my heart to pain when I was a child. Before closing my heart to my parents, it would have broken even if someone even killed a bug. Now that my heart is opened again, I have a heightened sensitivity and I feel the loss of everyone I have loved deeply.

Chapter
Thirty

AFTER WORKING FOR SEVERAL months in the Digital Equipment Springfield plant, I received a telephone call late one night from Henry Crouse, a man I had previously worked for. Out of the blue he told me that he was in love with me. This came as a shock. I asked him if he was drunk? He said he had been drinking but he was not drunk. We had a long conversation about what was going on in his life and why he thought he was in love with me. He answered that he fell in love with me the day he interviewed me three years ago. He also said he was married and did not need any problems.

I called him the next day and jokingly asked if he wanted me to erase the tape. We both laughed and he said "no." After talking with him further, I learned that he had been passed over for the position he had expected. This was especially painful because one of his peers had received the promotion. I told him that he did not need an affair, what he needed was a friend.

We continued talking for the next several months. One time he came to Springfield on business and took me to dinner. He invited me back to his room for a nightcap. After fixing me a drink he told me to take my shoes off. I asked why and he said I should get comfortable. I told him that I didn't need to get comfortable and proceeded to put my coat on. He looked startled. I don't know what he planned, but I was not having any of it, and just waited at the door until he got his coat to take me home. I know this sounds naïve, but I took him literally when he invited me back to his room for a drink. And I really thought he just wanted us to have a drink and talk. Nevertheless, I was not going to be used as a consolation prize for his missed promotion.

Since I was a child, I have always played the protective role of my parent, and in this role, I knew it was not wise to have an affair with a White married man, who was an executive at the place I worked.

The following week, during a meeting in Chicago, Henry met Don, someone that I had known professionally for a long time. Don asked him if he knew me.

"Yes," Henry said. "I know her very well."

"So, why didn't you bring her with you?" Don asked.

Henry said he didn't bring me because he didn't want to get into trouble. This was probably not a truthful answer.

"You won't get into any trouble with her," Don assured him.

Henry called me when he returned to Boston and shared his encounter with Don.

He said to me, "You have a good reputation out there."

This really impressed him and increased his interest in me.

What I learned? Protect your professional reputation, men talk.

Chapter

Thirty-One

*A*FEW MONTHS LATER, HENRY called me and said he wanted to come to Springfield to talk to me. I was very curious, and tried to imagine what was on his mind.

Henry hired me into the company, and we always had a very close professional relationship. But that was all it was. So when he came to my apartment that evening and told me the nature of what he wanted to discus with me, I was more than a little shocked. "I want us to have a relationship." I said, "what?" You can imagine someone you had never even kissed saying this to you. So, I went into my counseling role. "What is happening in your life? You are the most straight and conservative person I have ever known."

Henry was what one would describe as the perfect boy scout: dutiful, respectful and responsible. At this point in his life, he had never even gotten a traffic ticket. And here he was proposing to having an affair and/or a relationship with a black woman who worked for a company where he was not only an executive, but was one of the first employees hired at Digital Equipment Corporation as the assistant to the president. Badge number 26.

"I am unhappy, and plan to divorce my wife. We have nothing in common other than our children. We have grown apart, and don't share similar interests. I find our social group very boring, and the games they play at parties juvenile. I don't see how my marriage can survive, there is nothing there for me. I am going to leave, I just need to put some things in order.

"I think you and I look at life through the same window, and I think you can make me happy. I know you will help me to live longer. I just need to know that you will wait for me. There are some things I have to do before I leave. I told him, that I don't want to risk my livelihood, and I have a lot to lose if I got involved with him. I would be the one to suffer any consequences. Henry was very honest with me that evening. He said, " if I waited for him and we had a relationship, I might not be able to marry you because of the political fallout or blowback from my divorcing my wife and marrying a black woman." I just listened. This was all so surprising and shocking.

This was 35 years ago, and interracial marriages were still uncommon. I laughed when he asked, "if we move in together, what will we do in the evening?" Recovering from my shock, I said, "what we would do in the evenings, is a very minor problem. How we would make this relationship between two intimate strangers work, might be the major issue?"

Henry and I talked for several hours, with him doing most of the talking, and me listening.

"You will have to leave the company. What will you do you then?" he asked.

"I always wanted to finish college."

"Then that is what you should do." Henry said this like it was an official statement.

I spent a week reflecting on Henry's proposal. And thought myself crazy to even be considering it. I am a very intuitive person, and something told me that this was the right thing for me to do. As in the past when confronted with a confusing or muddled situation, I relied on my gut as my internal guide but in this case I sought the professional advice of a psychologist. The offer of completing my college education was tempting, but contained many pitfalls.

As was usual, when I need a professional I consulted the yellow pages. The first person who responded to my call that was pleasing to me, was the person I made the appointment to see. In this case it was Paul Allen, a psychologist, whose office was not far from where I worked.

"How can I help you?" Dr. Allen asked after our introduction.

I gave him a brief history of Henry and my relationship. Which included Henry's surprising proposal.

"Why is this a problem for you? It appears that you don't really know each other."

"That's a big part of the problem." We never even kissed." I answered. And in addition, "If I accepted Henry's offer, and broke up his marriage, I think the God's would punish me."

I continued to answer Dr. Allen's questions about me, Henry and our circumstances.

He asked about my childhood, my recent separation from my husband, and why Henry's offer to share his life with me was appealing?

I told him about my unhappy childhood, and about my unhappy marriage. And even thought I did not know Henry romantically, I trusted him. "Why do you trust him?" Dr. Allen asked.

"I attended a management workshop a couple of years ago. The workshop contained a series of exercises that elicited answers that revealed our deepest fears, desires, and professional objectives. What was most surprising to me was my answer to the question, who is important to you in your work life? Without any hesitation I wrote, Henry Crouse. This startled me because I was not conscious of this."

After the workshop ended I spent time reflecting on my answer and why Henry had such professional significance for me? As I thought about it and replayed the time when I worked directly for him, I realized that Henry responded to me like my father responded. Like my father, he never said no to me when I really wanted something. In addition, I found an important and more significant connection to Henry during a management development workshop. It came from an exercise designed to reveal what was most important to you in a romantic relationship - love, security, intelligence, beauty, or personality. I scored very high on security.

My sharing this with Dr. Allen made it clear to both of us why I was interested in forming a relationship with Henry. Henry made me feel secure because he spoilt me like my father, and he could financially support me while I at least completed college.

"Now I understand your attraction to Henry's offer."

"I understand better, myself. My only hesitation is my guilt over being responsible for Henry's leaving his wife, and the fear of the Gods punishment."

"Claudette, I don't think you need a psychologist. I think you had clarify around this issue." "But what about the Gods?"

"We all do things that may anger the Gods that is human behavior. I suggest you spend time getting to know Henry, and then make your decision. But I am always here if you need me."

"Dr. Allen, thank you so much. Our talk has been very helpful."

I took his advice and got to know Henry and decided to accept his proposal. In terms of my fear of the gods punishing me, I trusted I would be forgiven.

And knowing Dr. Allen was there if I needed him, gave me the assurance, and I signed on with Henry, left the company, and enrolled in school. Our relationship then and now, fulfilled the warlock's prophecy.

What I learned? An affirmation of the words in the poem "Waiting"— "Those I am seeking are also seeking me." Sometimes you have to step out on faith and trust the Gods will be forgiving.

Chapter

Thirty-Two

𝓔VEN WITH ALL THE assurances, I was still hesitant about getting romantically involved with Henry. It wasn't only the fear of being punished by the God's. My concerns were more worldly than being punished by the Gods. Did Henry really mean what he said about providing for me while I completed college? What would happen to me if I quit my job and our relationship ended?

Security was very important to me, so I didn't rush into accepting Henry's proposal. I did take Dr. Allen's advice that I should get to know Henry and then decide. Because we lived in different cities, we didn't see each other often, but talked on the phone every day. My asking him all kinds of questions, when did you first fall in love? And other questions far too personal to print in his book.

Trust was another important issue for me. And I was reassured when Henry answered all my questions. Very unlike my former husband, George, who felt under attack if I asked him anything that was personal. I am not sure if Henry answered my questions truthfully, but it was important that he was open to me, and trusted me enough to share his intimate feelings and thoughts.

After a few months, I invited Henry to dinner at my apartment in Springfield. By this time I trusted Henry enough to accept his proposal. But I had not told him. After dinner he kissed me, and something magical happened. It was just a kiss, but that kiss was the confirmation that Henry was the person I had been seeking. I went from a place of uncertainty to complete confidence in Henry and in a future with him.

Henry was startled with my sudden turn around. Asking me why after not signing up with him for months, I now had this change of heart?

"I don't know." I answered. "I just know when you kissed me on my neck it just felt right, and complete."

"Alright, does this mean you are going to leave the company?"

"Yes." I answered.

"Do you plan to apply to college?"

"Yes."

"Which college?"

"I am not sure. I thought about applying to the University of Massachusetts, Boston."

"Okay, apply."

I applied to UMass, and after I was accepted, I began to plan for my new life, and spent the next few weeks going around my apartment yelling to the top of my voice I LOVE HENRY, all the while listening to Phoebe Snow singing "Poetry Man."

I left my job at Digital at the end of June, and moved to an apartment in Brookline, Massachusetts. That summer was the best of my life. I was free to do anything with nothing I had to do. Classes didn't start until September, so I had the entire summer to myself. It was a joyous feeling. It was the first time I was so free and I was happy, very happy. I spent time going to museums, visiting friends around the country, and traveling with my sons. This was a fun time. We went to New York City, Philadelphia, and Disney World.

My son George, (we call him Chuck) and I drove from Boston to Disney World. My son Garry (we call him Skip) joined us later, after he completed a course in summer school. Chuck and I had a bit of an adventure on our drive to Florida. After visiting in Philadelphia, we continued our trip driving to Fayetteville, North Carolina where we stopped for the night.

We were up early the next morning, and after eating breakfast, I volunteered to take the first leg of the drive. Chuck gave me instructions to follow route 195-South until I reached Daytona Beach, Florida. After giving me instructions he got into the back seat to take a nap. As I drove I continued to see signs to Daytona Beach by taking route One-South. I though this must be a shortcut that Chuck did not know about. Thinking I would surprise him, I turned off route 195-South onto route One-South. It turned out Route One-South was a local road with a local speed limit, which I neglected to notice. I was not on the new road 15 minutes before I saw a police car with flashing lights behind me.

"Chuck, Chuck, wake up, the police of after me." Chuck rose up in the back seat, and said, "Mom, don't stop, outrun him."

Of course, I stopped. The policeman approached and asked if I knew how fast I was going.

"No." I replied sheepishly."

"You were driving 55 miles an hour in a 35 mile-per-hour zone," he stated.

After looking over my driver's license and registration card. He said I had to pay a $100 fine. I gave him cash, and he was on his way. He didn't give me a ticket so there was no record of the transaction. It might have added to his salary for that week.

"Let me drive." Chuck said to me in a bossy tone. We switched places, him behind the wheel, and me in the back seat.

"Don't you get a ticket while I am sleeping like I did when you were sleeping." I admonished him.

I had hardly laid my head down before I heard Chuck scream.

"Mom, Mom, wake up the police are after me."

"Oh, don't stop, outrun them." I counseled him, just as he had counseled me.

I raised a smart child, and Chuck pulled over and stopped. He rolled down his window as the policeman approached.

"Hey boy, don't they have any speed limits up there in Massachusetts?"

"Yes sir," Chuck responded.

Thank God he was polite. After harassing Chuck a bit more, the policeman fined us another $100, which we paid in cash, and we were on our way.

"At this rate, Chuck, we are not going to have any money by the time we get to Disney World." I said to Chuck as I observed the policeman sauntering off with our money.

We did eventually arrive at Disney World where Garry joined us. He got a big laugh when I relayed the story of Chuck telling me to outrun a North Carolina policeman. The three of us had a great time enjoying the park and our time together.

After a wonderful summer with my sons, I started classes that September at the University of Massachusetts, Boston. Saying I was excited and thrilled to have the opportunity to complete my undergraduate degree, would be an understatement. I was filled with joy and grateful to Henry for providing me this wonderful opportunity. Being a 30-year-old student was a bit scary, but both the faculty and the students were receptive to older students because we made up a large part of the student population. I majored in Psychology and I had fabulous professors. The three professors who were my favorites, were Claire Golomb, Augusto Blasi, and Bernard Kramer. They were all superior teachers and made the study of psychology both exciting and applicable. They might have been my favorites because all three took a special interest in me, and encouraged me to continue my education in psychology and obtaining an advance degree.

Dr. Blasi was one of my favorites not only because he was a great teacher, but because I had developed a strong crush on him. The crush was so strong that I experienced withdrawal pains when the semester ended and I would not see him for the entire summer. I was suffering so much emotionally that I bought it up to Henry.

"Henry, I have a problem, and I need your help."

"Okay, what is it?"

"I need to talk to you not as my lover, but as my friend."

"All right, what is it?"

"I have a terrible crush on Dr. Blaisi, and I don't know how to deal with it."

"That's interesting, how can I help?"

"I don't know. Let's talk"

After Henry and I went round and round on my crush on Dr. Blasi, without any resolution, I said I am going to call Dr. Blasi to see if he can help. It was about 10:00 at night when I called him.

"Dr. Blasi, this is Claudette Pendleton. I have a problem I hope you can help me with."

"I will try."

"Dr. Blasi, I have a strong crush on you, and I am confused because I think I love Henry, and I need help understanding my feelings."

"We have crushes on people usually because of one, or more characteristics: they are intelligent, attractive, or fun. But we love people who may have the above characteristics and things that are profoundly deeper: they make us feel safe, we trust them, and we have a deep emotional connection to them."

"Okay. I understand this, but how do you know you love someone, I asked?"

"Just imagine not ever seeing that person again, how would you feel?"

"I got it, thank you. I have a crush on you because you are intelligent, handsome, and interesting. But I know I love Henry because he makes me feel safe, I trust him, and I would be devastated thinking I would never see him again. But what should I do with my crush on you?"

"You can just have it, he said"

"I can just have it?" I asked

"Yes, you can just have it," he repeated reassuringly.

I used his advice for the rest of my life. That you don't have to do anything with emotions or desires. You can just have them.

"Dr. Blasi, thank you so much. You are so smart, and wonderful.", I said to him as we ended the conversation.

Of course, Henry was waiting in the next room to hear the results of our conversation. I relayed the conversation to him verbatim. Henry is very cool, he made no comment after I told him everything that had been discussed. But I am sure he must have been relieved.

Another of my professors, Dr. Kramer said I had a special gift for psychology. He asked me what I planned to do after completing my undergraduate degree, I told him I planned to go to graduate school.

"Claudette," he said, "you are very bright with a very large personally, and you need to go to a school compatible with your gifts."

He then said he was going to take me to meet Dr. Charles Willie, Dean of the Harvard's Graduate School of Education. He told me that there was a program there in Consulting Psychology, and that I should submit an application. After our conversation, he took me to meet Dr. Willie, telling him about me, and sharing that I was applying for the Counseling Psychology program. It came as no great surprise that with that level of support, I was admitted to the program.

Attending Harvard was one of the peak experiences of my life. Up until that point, I had lived and worked in many different cities—both national and international—but I had never met so many stimulating, intelligent, and exciting people as I met when I was at Harvard. The professors were exceptional—passionate about their subjects, and they conveyed an excitement about their specialty that was captivating, and excitement that proved contagious to the students. They were enthusiastic and engaging, and provided opportunities for independent research, as well as experiential, and applied learning outside of the classroom. The courses were dynamic and the lectures were so inspiring that oftentimes the students would give the instructors standing ovations.

The two psychology professors who had the greatest impact on me were Drs. Lee Perry and Harry Lasker. I confess that I adored them, and was so in tune with Dr. Lasker by the end of the semester that I could complete his sentences. Dr. Perry and I had a special connection. She became an advisor and mentor to me. I learned many of life's lessons from her outside of the classroom. I was and continue to be inspired by her. Her subject was the "self," and her lectures were like poetry. They left her students with a profound understanding, and a passion for the subject. Dr. Lasker's course was on adult development. The quality of the lectures, the relevance of the knowledge, and the application of the subject matter exceeded my expectations. They provided a psychological foundation for me to use personally and professionally for years to come.

Dr. Lasker's course on adult development helped me to understand and become more tolerant of people who saw things differently than I did. His work was based on the research of Jane Loveinger whose research I'll make an attempt to explain accurately. What I remember from the course is that adults view the world and behave in ways that is dependent on their respective maturity level. This includes how they see, understand, and interpret the world. The levels are numerically ranked, and range from level 2.5 to level 4.5. The people at the highest levels possessed a broader and more liberal view of the world—one might say, a more enlightened view and a greater sense of generosity and humanity. People intuitively form friendships and relationships based on the proximity of their maturity level, and are drawn to those with levels close to or matching their own. Organizations and groups operate on this same principle—they have levels. People who are not at the organization's level get screened out before they can join. If by chance they are not screened out prior to becoming a part of the group, they are later driven out or quit the group.

To emphasize this point, Loveinger's researcher conducted an experiment that began with leaving 100 strangers alone in a room with one another for an hour. When the researcher returned, the 100 strangers had formed informal groups based on or near their levels. The research used a questionnaire and the subjects' answers were used to determine their maturity levels.

An exciting aspect of this course was discovering how our lives follow different themes depending on our ages. The students in Dr. Lasker's class ranged from 21 to 41 years of age. We were divided by sex and age into groups to test the theory. The theme for women in Group I, ages 21 to 29, was looking for the Mr. Right. The theme for women in Group II, ages 30 to 39, was that they had found Mr. Right, but he turned out to be Mr. Wrong and the dream became a nightmare. The majority of the women in the class were in Group II—they were divorced and attending graduate school to focus on their careers and professions. The theme for the women over 40, in Group III, was that they were either staying or moving on. They had examined their lives and made decisions to either stay married or get divorced. They were the happiest, most optimistic, and most contented group. The second happiest group was Group I— they were optimistic about their future and finding their love connection.

As a member of Group II, I realized after speaking with other women in the group that we all suffered from disappointment that our lives had not turned out as expected, and we were untethered—without a foundation. We didn't know where we were going or how we would get there. If I had to put it in one word it would be a feeling of insecurity. But we were making a new start on a new road to freedom and independence.

Although I was a member of Group II, I had the optimism of Group I. I was looking forward to finding happiness in both my professional and personal life. I had completed my master's degree in a profession I loved and I was engaged to a man I loved. The future seemed bright, and a long way from my unhappy childhood, and disappointing early marriage.

I left Harvard with a deeper understanding and appreciation for myself, a greater tolerance for others, and a lasting and profound curiosity to understand the people and the world around me. Coupled with an expectation that I could use my power and create the kind of life I wanted.

What I learned? Acquiring knowledge is the bedrock of self-actualization.

Chapter

Thirty-Three

$\mathcal{M}$Y TIME AT HARVARD was so intellectually stimulating, and fulfilling that I didn't want to leave, and applied for a place in the doctoral program for the coming year. Henry was not pleased and did not support my decision.

"This was not part of the plan." He said when I told him about my applying to the doctoral program.

"I know, but this is what I need if I want to work in field of psychology." I responded.

"I might not be accepted. They only accept a few students. Why don't we wait and see what happens. If I get accepted, we can decide then if you want to continue supporting me in this effort?"

Henry agreed.

As things turned out, they split in the baby in half. I wasn't accepted into the doctoral program, but I was accepted to come back the following year into the Certificate of Advanced Graduate Studies program.

Participating in this program would allow me to stay at Harvard and continue studying with my professors, and would enhance my chances of being accepted in the doctoral program the following year.

If I accepted this place, and then a place in a doctoral program it would mean I would be a student for at least four or five more years. This was not acceptable to Henry, and I was not thrilled with the idea of returning to Harvard the next year on the chance of getting into the doctoral program later.

I did apply to other doctoral programs, and was invited to come in for an interview for a place in the doctoral program at Boston University, but I wanted to be at Harvard, and turned down the interview.

What to do now? As I pondered my options, I could work in the counseling field. But the salaries were so low I would not be able to financially take care of myself. And I was not sure where my relationship with Henry was heading. It had been three years since I left working at Digital. When I told Henry I was applying for a job there, for some reason, his earlier fear about my working there and dating him had dissipated. Or maybe his wanting me to have a job overrode any fear of how the company would respond to our relationship.

I applied and was hired as a human resource representative in what was called the Coates Building, In New Hampshire. It was comfortable and familiar, and I adjusted quickly. I don't think many people at the company were aware that Henry and I were seeing each other. In any case I didn't tell my colleagues.

Working was not nearly as taxing as being a student, and I found I had a lot of free time to focus on my career, my relationship with Henry and myself. Digital provided a lot of opportunities for advancement, so I felt confident about my professional future. My relationship with Henry was going forward, but without a proposal of marriage. And then there was me.

My psychology courses had triggered memories of my unhappy childhood and opened old wounds. The psychology courses taught me that most people grow up with unfinished business from childhood. I spent time focusing on my emotions and reading books on overcoming childhood trauma. Healing was important to me because in my relationship with Henry I often overreacted to things that he said or did. For instance, if he promised to do something for me, and forgot, I would be deeply hurt, far more than the offense would warrant. I traced this back to my mother, not being reliable. I could never trust her to do what you promised.

Having this insight I wanted to be aware of more of the triggers that caused me problems in our relationship because I was thinking of marrying Henry. Although later I learned, Henry was not thinking of marrying me.

But in any case, working on myself became my major focus. I employed many of the strategies that were recommended in the books I read: accepting ourselves as we are; forgiving ourselves for not being perfect; and rejecting the internal critic.

I learned that lack of self-esteem comes from the early conditioning when our parents repeatedly tell us to be nice, to share our toys with others, and it is not good to be selfish. Somehow these messages tell us that what we want is not as important as it is to be nice. This is the beginning of our not feeling worthy, especially if you are a girl. Many of our problems will be the result of our lacking in self-esteem

By the time I was in my teens I had an independent streak, and new the price of doing what other people wanted me to do, was too high. Although my mother's ill treatment of me, damaged my self-esteem, my father's acceptance must have balanced it out. I have always gone my own way, but with the wrong attitude. Being rebellious was as damaging to my self-esteem, and self-worth as being obedient or submissive. I existed in a constant state of battle of resistance. One would probably say I was stuck in adolescence even though my behavior persisted through my adulthood.

For whatever reason I resisted the acculturation that was directed at girls.

Although both boys and girls are taught to be polite, girls are also taught to be "nice." Where boys are encouraged to be assertive and aggressive, girls are encouraged to be passive, and compliant. If they are not compliant they are penalized. We see evidence of this in the United

States Armed Forces. When women complain when they are raped, they are often the ones punished, not the rapist. And for those of us who have worked in corporate America, we have witnessed the retribution many women have faced when they have asserted themselves. Even by other women. A case can be made that this is why many women did not vote for Hillary Clinton in the last presidential election. Both men and women found her to be too assertive. Too confident. The stakes are often high, and it is made clear from childhood that girls and women need to stay in their lane, If they want the approval and acceptance of their social groups: family, work, community.

Thus, it is not hard to understand why so many women struggle to gain self-approval and to be their true selves. They often lack the ability or courage to say what they want, and what they don't want, or to be direct and forthright. When they assert themselves, they get direct feedback that they are aggressive, pushy, and when older, the b---- word.

A Digital manager once said that when I sat across from him, I always looked him directly in the eye. When I heard this, my response was, "Where did he want me to look? His crotch?"

Early on in our relationship, Henry and I had an argument, and I told him what I honestly thought about him. That he was cheap, passive aggressive and closed minded. He said I wasn't being nice. I told him that being nice was not my goal— my goal was to be honest. What precipitated the argument, was I picked him up the airport and he got behind the wheel. He stopped for gas, and as the attendant was putting gas in the tank, Henry suddenly jumped out of the car to tell the gas attendant not to fill the gas tank up. This infuriated me. "Henry, you don't have to put gas in my car. I can fill my tank myself. One thing I hate is a cheap man." I then went on to tell him all the other things that pissed me off. I think the phrase is gunny sacking, or dumping. After emptying my sack, I explained to Henry that our relationship had to be built on honestly.

If we were going to truly get to know and accept each other, we needed to tell each other the truth. We have been married over thirty years and my directness is still a bit of an issue. For me, having the courage to be honest is one of my highest values. It is a way for me to be true to myself.

Chapter
Thirty-Four

$\mathscr{A}$T THIS TIME IN my life, I was feeling more confident. I had ended an unhappy marriage, completed under graduate and graduate school. Building on these successes, I was prepared to take on my next challenge. To find out what were the obstacles to my happiness? Or to my internal security?

I knew if I wanted to achieve my goal of being comfortable in my own skin, and to accept myself fully and had to continue on the road to self-discovery. For anyone who knows me, they know when I set a goal, I become centrally focused in pursuing that objective. I purchased and read more books. I kept a journal, and sought out a therapist. All were directed to self-inquiry to understand who I am, and accept myself warts and all. I now had the skills and the courage to look inside and find what is there: what made me happy, what made me sad, what was my greatest fear, what were my hopes and dreams? What were my true motivations, what drives me? I had always tried to avoid my feelings. Now my goal was to connect to them. I was looking for my authentic self. My objective was to be truly at home in my own skin. To be confident in who and what I am. Without apology.

Allison Tibbs writes in her book *Self-Acceptance*, that loving yourself is the first step to getting the things you want from your life. She suggests that you make a decision to practice loving yourself. Turn your critic off in your head when you are being self-critical. "Instead, say self-affirmations. Affirm that you love yourself because you are worthy of love, and avoid people who put you down or make you feel devalued."

In my quest for self-acceptance I tried to integrate her advice. Avoiding people who put me down or who made me feel devalued was my biggest challenge if they were female and were my friends. I tried understand why this was so. And traced it back to my mother who always put me down. So I was drawn to this type of female friends just like battered women are often drawn to men who batter them.

As I was struggling with this phenomena, another book titled *Thick Face Black Heart* by Chin-Ning Chu was extremely helpful. In her book, she says one must be vigilant in protecting one's self worth. I lived the following segment on a daily basis. There are people who come into your life as friends, but who are in fact your intimate enemies. They pretend to love you and to have your best interests at heart. But once you let them in, they become the thief of your peace and serenity. She says to keep a respectful distance from them. They operate by thriving on their own inferiority. They are insecure, don't like who they are, are envious of others, and feel better when they control and hurt people who make them feel small. Their actions and words are cutting even if you're nice to them. Actually, they are cowards. On the one hand, they play up to the ruthless and cunning types who treat them like dirt, and yet they are mean to people who are decent and kind to them. The serenity stealers make off with your heart and confidence with their sweet, charming exteriors. But after you let them get close to you, they will attack you in order to diminish you. These people are makers of "death by a thousand cuts." You should always keep them at arm's length. When you have a high self-esteem it is easier to accomplish this.

It took me a long time, and hours of pain and tears before I got to this point. For I was often with friends who constantly made me feel bad by being critical of everything I said or did. Sometimes they made direct attacks on my character. Sometimes it was on the way I looked or how

I dressed. Intuitively, I knew their attacks were generated by envy. But I was confused because I thought they were friends. I spent many days questioning if you could like someone that you envied? And I still don't have the answer. And still struggle to some extent with this issue.

An example, a close friend called and told me she had brain cancer. Normally, I am the person doing all the talking, but I could tell she was frightened, and listened attentively as she related how the doctor discovered the cancer, how they planned to treat her, and her prognosis. She talked for over two hours, with my interrupting to ask questions for clarification. I just wanted to comfort her because I knew she was upset and worried.

I called her to check in with her a few days later, and instead of thanking me for being a friend and listening to her, she put me down.

"Girl, I can't believe for once you let me do the talking. Normally, I can't get a word in."

I think this snide remark came from a place where she wanted to strike out at me because she felt she had revealed a weakness, and thus in a lower position. The illness and her leaning on me made her feel too vulnerable, and thus she had to attack as a way of repositioning herself. At least this is how I analyzed it. But it stung me.

As I progressed in my reading, therapy, and self-discovery, I found all of these of attacks share a similar pathology: You have something they wish they had, and they attack you for having it. I read in one of psychology books that envy is the most heinous of all emotions because it wants to destroy and annihilate the object of their envy.

As I said, I remain confused, because the same people who hurt me, are the same friends who help me, especially when I am in difficult circumstances. How can one care enough about you to help you, but often hurt you? Sometimes verbal with criticism, and sometimes by excluding you from social gathering just to make you feel left out.

Reading *Thick Face, Black Heart* explained this clearly and helped me to manage myself in my relationships with these women so they could no longer hurt me. I learned to keep them at an emotional (and literal) distance. Being free from their attacks and from my own constant questioning as to whether the source of the conflict was them or me, was a great lift to my self-esteem.

In time, I was able to be with them, and to assert myself in situations when they attempted to put me down. This new behavior was initiated by a telephone conversation I had with a woman who said to me, when I disagreed with her,

"Now don't come over here and curse me out."

"Why would I come over and curse you out?" I responded.

"Everyone always asks me has Claudette cursed you out?" She answered.

It was then I realized that when I let people abuse me to the point that I lashed out, they accused me of cursing them out. Which I had not done, but I had screamed and yelled. I said to myself, you have given your enemies a weapon to use against you, and now you must take it back.

From that time on, more than 20 years ago, I have not let people provoke me until I reached a boiling point. Instead when someone said or did something to me that I didn't like, I responded to them in the moment. I tried to nip attacks in the bud, and not let people get away with saying mean and nasty things to me until I lost my temper.

After that I took every new incident as an opportunity to practice assertiveness, and my new behavior of responding in the moment. One particular time a friend attacked me after a meeting because the board voted to support my proposal and not hers. After the meeting she accused me of buying the vote because of the large donation I had made to the organization, and she made other nasty comments about my buying my way into other groups. I calmly told her that it was not my donation that influenced the outcome, but my proposal was sound, was based on good ideas and good research. She was surprised at my demeanor. In the past I would have gotten angry and responded in a loud outburst.

I read a poster that said, "No one can put you down without your consent." I think this means you should not let other people have control over how you feel or how you respond.

As I said becoming fully who you are is a process. Sometimes you go a few steps forward and sometimes you slip back a step or two. But the important thing is to continue to become more of who you are.

This was all an approach to positive change, to creating the kind of person I wanted to be so I could have the kind of life I wanted to have. I continued reading and searching for answers to help me with my goal of fully being me. A book by Sharon Anthony Bower and Gordon H. Bower, offers a guide to positive change, which gave me added confidence to confront and be honest with people when they invade my space, are rude, or ask me for something that I don't want to agree to. They suggest when we don't stand up for ourselves, we are not taking responsibility for the quality of the kind of relationship we want to have with that person. By learning to be assertive, we are learning self and relationship management. Learning to stand up for our rights without stepping on the rights of others is imperative to managing ourselves with others.

On my journey to finding my true self, I tried to apply the lesson from a poem from the *Tibetan Book of Living and Dying*, where one must learn to avoid a deep hole in the sidewalk. In a sense my childhood was a deep hole and all my efforts to grow, and develop into a confident person, are based on efforts to get out of this deep hole. And when by chance I fell back in, I had to discover which strategy to use to get out of the hole, and in time, to avoid falling in altogether.

According to Bower and Bower, learning to be assertive is a process. And it takes practice and commitment to wanting to grow and change. They suggest that you write a script for different situations where you want to be assertive and that you rehearse these scripts with the right tone and body language until they become very natural and familiar.

They say this approach is useful in interpersonal situations and with people with whom you have conflict.

The following tip from a friend was most helpful to me. She said to write down what you want to say so that you don't get flustered and lose your effectiveness when in meetings.

In my own life, and with many of my friends who have difficulty in standing up for themselves, it was because we were not sure we had the right. We were taught in early childhood not to be selfish, to be nice. The result of this conditioning made it hard for us to ask for what we needed or to say "no" to someone who was stepping on our toes or invading our space, or our lives.

In her book, *Overcoming Childhood Trauma*, Christell Benson gives advice on emotional triggers from our childhood that cause problems in our adult lives. Reflecting on this I remembered a very hurtful and shameful incident when I was married to George. He and I were playing cards with a couple who were close friends. The woman and I got into a disagreement over a particular play that she made. I was a serious card player at the time.

"Why did you play that jack of spades?" I asked her.

"I played it because I wanted to," she answered.

"Well it was the wrong card," I responded.

She said she didn't care.

"Well I care, and if you don't then I don't want to play." I got up from the table. After I got up George picked up the cards and said to Joan, and Ale, let's play cut throat. This is a game where only three people play. I went into a rage and slapped George across the face. He was stunned.

"You are crazy!" he said.

My behavior shocked me, and I was embarrassed. I later learned that George wanting to continue to play cards with the couple without me triggered in me all the times when my mother took the other person's side whenever I had differences with anyone. She was never on my side. Her response when I had difficulty in a relationship was.

"Claudette I know you, you always want your own way. You are selfish and don't care about other people." I felt dismissed by George and betrayed. These were similar feeling that I felt with my mother. Reading the book I was able to identify some other triggers and I sought counseling after the following incident.

A girlfriend did something to make me angry. I started screaming at her at the top of my lungs, but this was an overreaction to whatever she did. So I knew something else was going on and I made an appointment with a psychiatrist. During the visit, while describing what happened between my friend and me, I suddenly realized that what she had done was very much like something my mother use to do to me. This was an ah-ha moment and an example of the triggers that Christell Benson wrote about.

Chapter

Thirty-Five

$\mathcal{A}$LTHOUGH RECOGNIZING MY TRIGGERS was a major step in my process of healing. I had a lot more work to do. I wanted to understand the genesis of childhood trauma, and I started to read books on parenting, self-esteem, and their impact on relationships. I read that good mothering is crucial to the emotional development of children. And the most important thing a parent can do is to love, nurture, and keep their children safe. They also need to provide limits and discipline, but the discipline must come from a place of love. They should never label their kids as being silly, lazy, or bad. Kids live up to or down to your expectations. What parents say to them sticks. So it is important for them to hear the positive things about who they are and what they can become. This all caused me to think about my mother and myself as a mother.

Reading this made me think of my sons—George and Garry. As a young mother, I repeated the mistakes of my parents. I did not nurture my sons enough. I never hugged or kissed them, or just cuddled up with them. This is my only life regret.

I learned children who have inadequate parenting often lack self-esteem, as I did. Overcoming the lack of self-esteem took a lot of reflection, learning, and effort. Receiving love and feedback from others was very important.

When I was a young adult, a wife and mother, I wasn't even sure what having self-esteem meant. Now I know the importance of self-worth and how closely it is tied to self-acceptance. It is to know you don't have to be perfect to be worthy, to be able act in your own best interest, and to stand up for yourself.

Becoming fully who you are can be a lifelong process, and I am grateful for the people who gave me the support I needed as I evolved. Henry has been a major part of supporting me in my journey of self-discovery. But he was not so supportive when I garnered enough confidence to confront him about marriage. It seems our future went a bit sideways. This was the situation. We had been living together for a year, and dated for more than three years. In my view this was enough time to gage whether we were compatible, or not. It seemed we were. This being the case, I thought it was time for us to get married. On a Sunday morning, I asked him when his divorce was going to be final.

His response was, "I never filed for divorce."

"You told me more than three years ago that you had gone to a lawyer to file for divorce," I said.

"The lawyer told me it would be better if my wife filed," he continued.

This came as a shock and I told him that I felt depressed.

"I wonder whom the Patriots are playing today," he said.

It was a very insensitive response.

After the shock of all this wore off, I went upstairs, packed a bag, and left the house. I called Henry from my motel room later that day and told him of my plans. The next day, I was going to get a 30-day furnished apartment. If he was divorced and we were married within the thirty days, our relationship would continue. If not, it would end. He said to give him time.

"You have used up all your time in the three years that you didn't file," I said to him.

After a lengthy conversation, he agreed that he would get divorced and marry me within my timeframe. Within the month, he had flown to Santo Domingo and gotten a quick divorce. Not long afterwards, we were married. We had two ceremonies. The first came on April 2, 1982 when I woke up one morning anxious that the marriage would not happen. Fretfully, I called Henry and asked him if he would marry me. He said that he already planned to marry me.

"I mean today," I said to him.

"Claudette," he said. "I am working and I can't marry you today."

"What about tonight?" I asked.

He said "Okay," and I immediately called my girlfriend and asked her to find a Justice of the Peace to marry us that evening. I also asked her to find a nice restaurant where we could go to celebrate. That Friday evening at 7 p.m., Henry and I were married with my son George, his friend Patrina, and our friends Lou, Michon, Maejim, and David all in attendance.

The second wedding occurred on April 10, as planned. It was a small wedding—only 50 friends in attendance. The ceremony, in the town house where we were living in Lexington, Massachusetts, did not go off without a hitch. The minister who was to marry us was more than two hours late. The guests were getting bored and restless waiting, so we opened the bar.

My girlfriend said, "This is the first wedding I have been to where they had the reception before the wedding."

After some more time had passed and the minister still a no-show, the best man called the Justice of the Peace who had married us earlier.

Everyone gathered around us. I still see the adoring faces all looking at us as we took our vows, promising to always love and care for each other. It was the peak of shared experience.

I had had two glasses of champagne before the ceremony and while the Justice of the Peace was admonishing us not to marry for sexual gratification, I chimed in and said, "No, marry for money."

He said, "Let me tell the jokes."

Henry and I both continued working at Digital after we married with some trepidation. Henry's employee badge was number 26, which meant that he was the 26th person hired by the company and was very close to president. The company had grown from 26 employees to 110,000 at that time and Henry was an important part of the senior staff. We were both concerned how the president or the management team would react to our marriage. A few interesting things happened after the wedding. A few interesting things happened after the wedding was announced. We were invited to attend Digital's "Night at the Boston Pops" with the board of directors and the executive committee. This was a big deal. The reception was held on Beacon Hill, at the home of General Georges Doriot, the "father of venture capitalism, and the person who provided Ken Olsen the seed money, to start Digital Equipment Corporation. Henry and I were seated at the head dinner table with the company's president, Ken Olsen, and I was placed next to Ken. I am sure this was by design so Ken could have the opportunity to assess this person whom Henry had recently married. Henry said during the early weeks of our marriage, Ken made frequent trips and stops in his office, and that this was the president's way of putting his arms around you when he thinks you might be in trouble. A year later Henry was transferred to the company's European headquarters in Geneva, Switzerland as Vice President of Manufacturing. I am sure there was a connection. The president of Digital was a very conservative man. He didn't approve of smoking, divorce, or any of the human frailties. I am sure it came as a great shock to him when he learned that Henry, one of his favorites, had divorced his white wife and married a Black woman. Early in his career at Digital, Henry was the president's assistant. Having a badge number of 26 and being the president's assistant meant he had a very special relationship and connection to Digital's President, Ken Olsen. So it was crucial to Henry's career for Ken Olsen to embrace and accept our marriage. The organization took his lead and Henry stayed at the company until he retired 10 years later.

My marriage to Henry was one of the most important and best decisions I ever made. He was the mother I never had—loving, nurturing, and kind. When I had a fever, he put me in the tub, wrapped me in a towel, and put me to bed. He always supported my decisions, and never put me down for my failures. If I am overwhelmed and overburdened, he takes over and completes my tasks. I have a busy social calendar, because I am always out networking to raise money for various causes. Sometimes I am too tired to attend an event, and Henry will often go in my stead. When we have a dinner party, and If I am exhausted, he will clean off the table and washes the dishes.

While I was studying at Harvard, a man from Nigeria wanted to date me. After refusing him several times he asked me why I wouldn't go out with him. I said I was already dating someone.

He asked, "What was so special about this guy?"

I told him what was special about this guy, was he allowed me to be myself, that he allowed me be free, and that he never tried to change or criticize me. He asked for further clarification. I said if I wanted to curse, like say, GD, he doesn't condemn me. The guy from Nigeria, said, "Oh no, I don't like to hear a woman curse."

I said, "See this is what I mean. He lets me be me." He got the message.

Many of my friends often commented on how surprised they were by Henry's acceptance and support for me. They saw me as difficult, spoiled, and too direct.

I remember his asking me once, "Why do Anne and Betty refer to me as a saint?"

This is the same Anne who had confided that she was very concerned about me when she first found out I was dating a white man. She told me she kept thinking, *I sure hope that white man doesn't hurt her.*

Smiling at me later, she said, "Now I know I should have been worried about Henry!"

Many of women are reluctant to tell their husbands when they wreck the car. I never have to worry about this. Henry only wants to know if I am alright.

Henry is a quiet man, the total opposite of me. He is not quick to anger, and he forgives easily. One would never expect him to act quickly or compulsively. He weighs every word before he speaks or answers. But once he gets to know a person, he displays charm, a quick wit, and rich humor. His major love is flying, having owned two airplanes. There have been many times he has flown us to different tourist places just to have dinner. I can say very confidently that Henry is a wonderful husband, and it has been exciting living with him. But I also tell my friends that being wonderful, does not mean being perfect. Henry is kind, but passive aggressive. His attacks are subtle and can be hard to recognize. An example came one night after I had stayed out late partying with friends. The next morning I was hung over. Henry brought me aspirin. Later that day we went out to dinner. Waiting in line to be seated, we joined in a conversation with a group of young college students. As the conversation progressed, Henry suddenly asked them how old they thought I was. This surprised them and me. They answered that I looked like I was 25, but I must be older because he was asking the question.

"She's 38," he said to them.

This was his punishment for my having stayed out late. Once I was not working and he thought I needed something to do.

"I have a job for you," he said.

"What is it?" I asked.

"To pick up the mail every day." This was his indirect way of saying, "You need to get a job."

I told my girlfriend this, and she told her husband.

He said, "What kind of job is that?"

After several weeks, Henry said, "I want to compliment you."

"On what?" I asked.

"On getting the mail every day."

If I happened to be on the phone talking to my girlfriends, and I had forgotten to get the mail, I would tell them I have to go and pick the mail up before Henry gets home.

"Where is the mailbox?" they would ask.

"At the end of our driveway," I'd reply.

A close friend, told me her daughter said to her, "Mother, when I grow up I want to marry a man like Mr. Crouse. Do you see how he treats Mrs. Crouse?"

My friend said she told her daughter, "I agree with you, I want to marry someone like Mr. Crouse too." We had a good laugh.

Henry and I share a special connection based on trust and love. During one of my psychology courses the professor stated that when we are trying to make a change in our personality it is important that someone holds us while we let go of the old self, and transition into the new self. Henry was the person who held me while I relinquished the old self who was distrustful of love or true intimacy. I was then able embrace the love he offered me. This also enabled me to trust him even though we might have demonstrated our love in different ways.

It was my birthday, and all of my friends and loves remembered and acknowledged my special day. Henry reserved a limousine and took several friends out to dinner with us to celebrate. We arrived home close to midnight, just before our telephone rang. It was M.L. and Sylvia Carr, calling to tell me, "We rushed home before twelve o'clock so we could wish you happy birthday." After we ended the call, I turned to Henry and said, "I am so happy, this was such a perfect day. Thank you. I love you so much, I would die for you. Would you die for me?"

He said, "under certain circumstances."

"What are they?" I pressed.

"At the moment, I can't think of any," came his frank response. I laughed so hard at his unexpected and truthful answer. My reaction is a reflection of how secure I am in Henry's love for me. He doesn't have to say he would to die for me to prove he loves me. He proves it every day in how he treats me.

Although our relationship ran into a wall when Henry was transferred to Geneva Switzerland, and I was told by the Digital Geneva management team that as a wife of a company executive I could not work there. When I wanted to challenge their decision, Henry said he did not want to fight with the people he had to work with. I saw my only option was to tell Henry that if I could not transfer and work at Digital Europe Headquarters, than I was not going. Things really heated up when Henry and I were at company functions and someone mentioned our transferring to Geneva, and I responded that I was not going. We eventually ended up in counseling. The therapist had Henry and I switch roles, and was surprised that we really saw and understood the other person's point of view, but maintained our positions on the issue of my working or not working, and my going and not going to move with Henry to Geneva if I could not work there.

My tactic finally paid off when Henry approached a colleague and explained our situation. "If I could not work for Digital in Europe, I was not going to move there with him. Henry's colleague was a very powerful Digital executive. Once he understood Henry's plight, he called the European President and told him that by not allowing me to work there because Henry would be on the executive team, would be unlawful in the United States. This approach proved to be effective and after the President of Digital Europe came to the States and interviewed me, he retracted his objections. I was told later that the manager who hired me paid the price, and was forced out of the company after a year or so as retaliation for going against the bosses and giving me a job.

Once this issue was resolved Henry and I were back to normal and were excited to move to Geneva. Although I had to walk on ice as everyone was watching my behavior and attitude. I just kept my head down and did my work. A few months after our move, I gave a party for the executive management team. The European Digital President brought his wife up to introduce me. He said, "I told you I had met an extraordinary woman, now you see what I mean." I guess I had made a favorable impression.

My boss questioned if my traveling 65 percent of the time would pose a problem for our relationship. I asked Henry if he thought this would be a problem.

"No, we will never have a problem," he told me. "We will always work it out."

I was happy to know that, since I didn't want to be staying at home with nothing to do while he worked and traveled. Most executive wives did not work. So I was an aberration, which is exactly which was fine with me.

What I learned? It is important to marry someone who loves you enough to accept you as you are, and helps you complete the unfinished business of childhood.

Chapter
Thirty-Six

*M*OVING TO GENEVA WAS nothing like my move to London, England twenty years earlier. Here I didn't speak the language. In Switzerland three different languages are spoken: French, German, and Italian, with French being the language spoken in Geneva. I am embarrassed to admit that after taking French in junior high school and college, and completing a four-week immersion course at *L' Institut de Francais* in Nice, France, I still could not understand or speak French. Fortunately, English was spoken at work, so there was no barrier to my accepting my new position. Language aside, Geneva was a beautiful and exciting city. It was international and many companies had their headquarters there. Its natural beauty derived from its location on the shores of Lake Geneva, surrounded by some of Europe's highest mountains. Before moving to Geneva, I always loved the ocean, but after living there the mountains became a close second.

Geneva is genuinely cosmopolitan, with the world's most expensive and beautiful clothes and jewelry stores (all dangerous temptations for me). Rue de Ronde is Geneva's version of Rodeo Drive. This was certainly my element, but at first I was too timid to enter the shops. With Henry's encouragement, I quickly snapped out of it, and still have some of the clothes I purchased more than twenty-five years ago. And still happily wear my Patek Philippe watch.

The Patek Philippe watch comes with a story. I fell in love with this watch when I saw it in a jewelry case at the Hyatt Regency Hotel in San Francisco, in 1980, but didn't buy it because after Henry saw the price, his look said *no*. At the time I didn't know that Patek Phillip watches are made in Switzerland, and are known throughout the world as watches of distinction.

It's surprising how well we read our mate's signals. Although, Henry didn't say in words not for me to purchase the watch, his body language, and his walking out of the store without me said, "Don't buy that watch."

Being the person that I am, I knew that there would be another day and another opportunity. This was early on in our relationship, and Henry was not yet used to my expensive taste. He said as much after he saw me purchase a pair of very expensive shoes, stating, "Is that how much shoes cost?" But it was not too long before he was encouraging me to buy the quality items that I love. Talk about influencing our mates!

Amazingly, the opportunity to purchase the watch appeared a few years later when we were sightseeing in Montreux, Switzerland. We happened upon a jewelry store, and I saw the watch in the jewelry store window and asked Henry to buy it for me as a Christmas present. He agreed. When Christmas came and I didn't receive the watch as a gift, I was very disappointed. When I asked Henry why he did not buy it for me, he said he went back to the store to buy it, but it was closed. I tried to make sense of why a store would be closed so near to Christmas. I came up with the answer—they must have been closed for inventory. A few months later, we went by the same store. I went inside and told the store clerk that my husband had been there just before Christmas and found the store closed.

He said, "Oh, we were closed for lunch."

Henry not buying me the watch, and giving me some fake excuse that the store was closed, hurt my feelings. Especially since I had given him advice that saved him $47,000 on federal income taxes. When he was presented with an extremely high tax bill, I insisted the accountant had made a mistake and that he should have find another accountant to check his taxes. When they did, they found that the first accountant had made a serious error in computing our taxes. So when Henry didn't buy me the watch after I had made such a great contribution, I thought I deserved the watch, and he was a jerk to not buy it for me. I took the matter to my girlfriends. When I told them the story of the taxes, and Henry not buying me the watch, they accosted him, saying he did not appreciate me, that without my input he would have paid so much more in income taxes, and what more would a girl have to do to get her husband to buy her an expensive watch? After this encounter, with my girlfriends, Henry finally purchased the watch for my birthday while we were on a trip to London, England.

My desire to have Henry buy the watch for me was not about the watch. I could have bought the watch for myself. It was about showing appreciation and valuing my input that saved him from paying the Internal Revenue Service thousands of dollars.

I later made the connection as fascination for me. I wanted it from the time I saw it in the Hyatt Regency in San Francisco more than four years earlier. It was important because it resembled the gold watch my father bought me when I was thirteen years old.

What I learned? The power of emotional and subconscious imprints.

Chapter

Thirty-Seven

$\mathcal{S}$HOPPING WAS NOT THE major highlight of living in Geneva, but clearly, it was a close second. The city is an elegant metropolis with an alluring charm——a city of wealth and elegance with a longstanding reputation for humanitarianism. It houses the European United Nations Headquarters, and other large international corporations. One can stay in a beautiful hotel on Lake Geneva, or dine in exquisite restaurants, or stroll in its beautiful parks, or visit its charming old town. The numerous museums, sumptuous restaurants and the wordiness of its inhabitants, made living there interesting and pleasurable.

We toured most of the surrounding cities—Annecy, Montreux, and Switzerland's capital, Lausanne. One of the greatest moments was skiing in St. Moritz.

The television program *60 Minutes* did a show on the Palace, one of most expensive hotels in St. Moritz. Henry told a friend that was where we were staying.

The friend replied, "You bastard."

While in St. Moritz, we made sure to visit the Palace Hotel to take pictures to send to Henry's friend.

What I learned? How to use the back of my ski boots to pull myself up after a fall and to enjoy skiing.

Chapter

Thirty-Eight

IT WAS EASY TO forget that the reason we moved to Geneva was because we had new jobs there. My role as European Logistics Human Resource and Training Manager was to lead and manage a European project team to build a Logistics Training Center in Nijmegen, Holland. As project manager, I led a team composed of logistics managers from all of the major digital subsidiaries in Europe: England, Germany, France, Italy, and nine smaller countries. I knew from past experience that my success depended on my being accepted by the team and by my colleagues on the executive management staff.

Henry, being on the staff of the president of Digital Europe, made my task more difficult. In Europe, executives are like gods and some people thought I would have too much influence because I was married to Henry.

Before the President of Digital Europe consented to my being hired, he interviewed me. He explained the culture at the Geneva Headquarters, adding that managers there had a lot of power over their employees, and how my being the wife of an executive and working there might cause a problem if I wanted to take advantage of my position.

I told him I had a strong sense of my own power and did not need to use the power or influence of my husband. This must have satisfied him, because he didn't oppose my working there.

Early on, I witnessed an example of the power of the bosses at our

European office. I was meeting with a manager when the man's superior called. Although he was on the phone, his body language and voice gave the impression of one standing at attention and saluting! I was startled by his extremely formal and deferential behavior, and knew my irreverent personality put me at great risk in this corporate environment

To stay out of trouble, I adopted the strategy of keeping a low profile, doing my job, showing up on time, not to having too much to say, and wait to be accepted.

Both the executive staff and the project team were constantly on the go, travelling to meetings all over Europe. When traveling, the group always ate dinner together and continued working on resolving issues. After dinner, we all convened in the bar to drink, talk, and discuss the issues further. Our boss drank vodka martinis, smoked cigarettes, and talked into the wee hours of the night. Being new to the team, I didn't want to be the first to leave so I often stayed until my boss was ready to leave. Many mornings I was hung over and didn't want to join the group for the 7:00 a.m. breakfast, but I knew not joining them was not an option if I wanted to become an accepted member of the team.

After several months of staying up late with my boss, and getting up early for breakfast with the group. one colleague said, "Claudette, I wish I had your stamina." If he only knew how much I was struggling.

Shortly after this comment, drinking one night at a bar in Munich, Germany another colleague said, "Claudette, you are one of us."

Success.

His comment was extremely important, because my effectiveness depended on the support from my colleagues. Our boss was insecure and changed his mind often on a whim, especially if he received any opposition to his decision.

When I shared Don's comment with Henry. "He said, "I am not surprised that you got accept to the club. You have great political skills and you are very smart and adept at getting what you want. A lot of people do not know that you have to wait to be accepted to the club, and they make the mistake of trying to push their way in, and they get rejected. Congratulations!"

With acceptance into the group, it gave me confidence when I had to challenge our boss Jack when he tried to take back a decision he had previously made. "I never said that," or "I never gave you permission to do that," he'd protest. "Yes you did." I would say, knowing now I would not be jeopardy because whomever was present when Jack made the decision would support or agree with me. Bob might say, "Jack you might not remember because you were in a hurry to get to Carlos's meeting, when you gave Claudette the okay to go forward the proposal."

It was not always easy to get around my boss's fickleness, my supporter had to be a colleagues who Jack respected and trusted. When I had the strongest support, I would then approach my boss asking for his decision on a particular issue, by first telling him that Larry or Bob or George, thought it was a good idea, and was in agreement with me that this was the right or best way for us to go.

What I learned? Being an insider and being accepted by the team can help you manage your boss.

Chapter

Thirty-Nine

$\mathcal{M}$ANAGING THE EUROPEAN PROJECT team was no walk in the park. Each country had its own personality and cultural differences. When planning a trip to a subsidiary, I had to design a different approach for each trip, depending on the country I was visiting. For England, my approach was to ask for help because the English were arrogant and thought they knew everything. When visiting France, I had to show patience and tolerance because the French were arrogant and never wanted to acknowledge there even was a Genevan headquarters. When visiting Italy, I had to tell them why I was there, what I needed, and go through each area in detail explaining the format and content of the work required. Visiting Germany was the easiest. The Germans respected authority and expected anyone from headquarters to tell them what the boss back in Geneva wanted them to do.

Henry and I both travelled more than 60% of the time, and went in opposite directions. Henry travelled mostly to England, Ireland and Scotland. I travelled mostly to Holland, Germany, and England. We attempted to synchronize our schedules when possible to be in the same place at the same time. But this was rare, and we only saw each other from Late Friday nights, Saturdays, and Sunday mornings. I always left for a trip on Sunday afternoons because I wanted to arrive at my destination during daylight. I had a great fear of being loss at night in a foreign county, not being able to speak the language, with the inability to communicate and find my hotel.

Another challenge that was confounding was trying to keep all of the country's personalities straight. My predecessor had given a project completion date before I accepted the job. My boss offered to extend the date, but I declined and said we would launch and open the new Logistics Training Center on schedule.

Our team met the deadline, but it took every ounce of energy I possessed. We met every week somewhere in Europe and worked day and night completing particular tasks. Henry's secretary after taking one look at me told him he should take me on vacation because she could see how tired I was even through my sunglasses.

The training center was built, furniture was delivered, the students were registered, and the teachers were assigned all on schedule. The only reason classes started two days after the designated project completion date was because it was a weekend. My boss was both surprised and impressed. He learned I was "more than Henry's wife." When he visited Digital headquarters back in Maynard, Massachusetts, I was told he bragged about me and told everyone I was doing an outstanding job.

What I learned? The way to earn a good reputation is by working hard, completing projects on time, and performing above expectations.

Chapter

Forty

$\mathcal{A}$FTER THE TRAINING CENTER was operational, I took on a new challenge that required more of my human resource skills. Our Logistics organizations had many open positions because of the company's rapid growth. It was difficult to find people with experience and skills in the discipline of logistics. The solution I offered was to promote and train women already in the organization. Promoting women into professional positions from clerical jobs was unusual in Europe during the 1980's, so we had a lot of unutilized female talent. I knew women could do some of the professional jobs with adequate training.

Being a woman and a human resource professional, it was important to me to advance the careers of women in our organization. My boss supported me in this effort, and his managers were instructed to identify and promote women with potential in their organizations. Which they did, and the number of women in professional positions increased to the extent that we were able to fill a lot of our open slots. And our recruitment problem was solved.

The company's rapid growth created even more opportunities for women and the entire management team including me. My boss directed me to conduct a job study to outline each of his teams' responsibilities to determine the appropriate salary levels and stock options for each manager. This was my first time participating in the stock option distribution program, and I felt like I had arrived as a senior executive.

At Digital we had matrix management (managers had two bosses), a functional boss, and an operational boss. My functional boss was responsible for Human Resources and my operational boss was responsible for Logistics. Each senior manager held their quarterly staff meetings in the most beautiful cities in Europe. Eight times a year, each team would meet in cities like Paris, Munich, Milan, London, and Spain. Where we held our meetings depended on the time of year and what was significant about that season.

What I learned? Executives received many corporate perks—travel, high salaries, and stock options. Which proves the adage, "It's great to be king."

Chapter

Forty-One

$\mathcal{H}$ENRY WAS HONORED BY the city of Galway, Ireland, on Galway's 500th birthday. He received this honor because he was the Vice President of Manufacturing and Digital was the largest employer in Ireland at that time. This was one of the highlights of our time in Europe. The celebration was held throughout the entire weekend. From a Friday night dinner through a Sunday morning breakfast.

Henry and I took the corporate jet to Ireland. Henry used the jet often, but it was my first time flying in luxury. We arrived just on Friday just in time to dress for a dinner that was hosted by John, a Galway Digital executive. The ten of us met for dinner at one of Galway's oldest pubs. After drinks we left John to pay the bar tab and went to the dining room. Not one to stand around and wait for long, I slide into the booth. Just as I arrived at the far end of the booth, one of the wives declared. "Oh, I think we should wait and let John seat us." Now, what should I do? Ignore her? No. With everyone watching, I slid out of the booth and waited with them for John to come and seat us. When I got the chance, I said to Henry, "Why didn't you rescue me by joining me in the booth? You are the guest of honor and can sit wherever you want." "And miss this opportunity to see how you were going to get out of this? Nope, I couldn't miss it." Henry knows how impatient I am, so he got a kick out of my self-inflicted discomfort.

We enjoyed dinner, drinks and the Irish humor.

Saturday morning after a good old Irish breakfast of eggs, English bacon, toast and marmalade, we were off to see the sights, and for me the shoops.

We returned to the hotel loaded down with packages of Irish linens, and Waterford crystal. We were surprised when it turned out that Henry's gift was comprised of boxes of Waterford crystal. So the Crouse's now had crystal glasses for any and every entertainment occasion. Back in our hotel room we changed quickly and dressed for the black tie dinner that was honoring Henry, and celebrating Galway's 500 Birthday. Henry and I were thrilled to participate in such an auspicious occasion, and Henry being the guest of honor made it even more special.

Entering the hall where the dinner was held took our breath away. It was magical, like being in fairyland. The decorations were magnificent with beautiful linens, exquisite floral arrangements, and exquisite place setting. Each place setting having beautiful Waterford crystal goblets and silver cutlery. I can't remember what was served for dinner, I was too overcome with the pageantry. There was a wonderful band and as soon as the music started, a handsome barrister came to our table and asked me to dance.

While twirling me around the dance floor, he said, "Charlie said you were lovely."

At the end of the evening, I told Henry the Irish were quite the charmers.

"There is a saying the Irish will charm the pants off of you," he said.

"Literally," I said.

After having breakfast Sunday morning, and saying goodbye to our hosts, loaded with our Waterford Crystal stemware and other items, we traveled on to Dublin. While we were waiting in the lobby to register, we were approached by an Irish gentleman who asked Henry if we had been in Galway the day before. Henry answered that we had.

This kind gentleman said to Henry, "I don't remember you, but I remember her." It is great when your husband hears these compliments about you from other men.

What I learned? I love the Irish charm and sense of humor.

Chapter
Forty-Two

BESIDES OUR SPECTACULAR WEEKEND in Galway, there was another time that Henry was an honored guest at a Digital event in London, England. He was invited by the Country Manager of Digital Europe to celebrate their annual airshow. Henry is a pilot so this honor had special significance for him. He was excited as a kid when pilots flew the vintage planes from the first and second wars. The weekend consisted of an airshow Saturday afternoon, a black-tie dinner Saturday night, and a brunch Sunday morning.

Both the dinner and brunch took place under a beautiful white tent. During dinner the weather abruptly changed, and we were in a massive thunderstorm. The rain flooded the tent and the guests. Everyone made due. The ladies removing their shoes, and the men rolling up their pants, and we partied on. Thank God by Sunday morning the weather had cleared in time for brunch in or the Prince Andrew and his fiancé Fergie to join us. One of her relatives worked with us in Geneva, and jokingly, I approached him asking if he could get us an invitation to their wedding. He laughed and said, "Claudette I would, but I don't have that kind of clout." I still have some of the photos taken of them at the brunch.

Our lives in Europe were full of exciting experiences. We were constantly going to beautiful and charming places. In Vienna we were lucky and got to see Luciano Pavarotti in *The Barber of Seville*. In Florence we purchased leather luggage from Italian monks. In Venice,

Rome, Amsterdam, Athens, and other cities we always found something special, and were captivated by their loveliness.

We met and had a special time with friends from the states when we traveled through Kenya. As the four of us, all people of color, drove through the areas where the Kenyans were living in mud huts, I reflected on my African ancestors and on what the women in these mud huts did at night. What were their thoughts? How did they feel about their circumstances and polygamy?

I was very touched by this experience. I felt a kinship with the inhabitants.

Years later, I watched a program on public television where they interviewed women from Kenya. They interviewed one family where the husband had four wives. When they asked the first wife how she felt when her husband brought the second wife home, she said the second wife was her sister, and that she left him and returned to her family. Her father beat her and made her go back to her husband. She said after that she became an alcoholic. He then married his third wife. When he married his fourth wife who was many years younger, the third wife left him and never returned. The fourth wife was asked why she married a fifty-two year old man when she was only twenty-three. She said it was because she had two children and the children's father would not marry her. I found this very enlightening. Up until that time I thought the wives were accepting of their husbands having multiple wives. The husband was a postmaster and I learned that as customary, he had to build a house for each wife. This was also a revelation to me. An African student told me that polygamy is one of the major reasons that Africa did not prosper. With each man having so many wives and children to house and educate there was never any inheritance left for his children, and each generation had to start from scratch.

Touring Kenya with our friends was a shared and joyful experience. We spent a week touring the national parks. After our friends left,

Henry and I stayed another week and traveled to lovely Mombasa on the Indian Ocean. Not knowing we had to confirm our flight from Nairobi to Mombasa, we couldn't take the 8 a.m. flight because we lost our reservations. And there were no seats available until 5 p.m. Having already checked out of the hotel, Henry wanted to rent a car and drive to Mombasa.

"No," I said. "We don't speak the language, nor do we know where the safe places to stop on the highway for refreshments are."

Henry is normally an easygoing person, but here he was recalcitrant. He insisted we rent a car and drive. After quarreling for a couple of hours, I suggested we rent a car and driver. Henry consented and a hotel doorman directed us to a car rental service. The Mercedes Benz came with a young driver. He told us the trip to Mombasa would take two hours. After driving for over an hour, our driver pulled into a service station. He and two young men walked around the car several times. Henry asked what was the problem. Our driver said the car needed a new plate for the engine and they were calling ahead for a replacement.

I told Henry that the guys didn't know how to repair a Mercedes and were just kicking the tires. Two hours passed and no plate had arrived. I told Henry I did not want to get stuck and have to spend the night out here in no man's land. I suggested we rent another car, but I forgot we were out in the boondocks, where no car rental agency exited. In response to my constant nagging, the young men told us a bus going to Mombasa would come through in an hour. It was ninety degrees outside. Even though we were dressed for the heat, in shorts and short-sleeved shirts, we were wet with perspiration, and our attitude was that hell couldn't be hotter than this. Although we were equipped with water, it didn't quench our thirst. We did use the water to wet a handkerchief to place around our necks. When the bus finally came, it stopped about two blocks from where we were. Poor Henry ran to the bus and asked the driver if he would take us to Mombasa. The driver asked how much luggage we had. Thank God Henry lied and said two pieces, when we had five. Henry came back and said the driver would come back and pick us up. I had little trust and insisted that we pay the young men to take our five pieces of luggage to the bus.

This was around 3:30 in the afternoon. The bus looked like the buses you see in developing countries filled with all kind of contraband, but to me it looked like a limousine. The conductor was not wearing shoes and had the dirtiest feet I had ever seen. The only seats available were two on the bulkhead, and not together. We drove until dark and the conductor started to speak to the passengers in Swahili. I finally figured out that he was asking where they wanted to be dropped off in their villages. I quickly realized that the places they were going to had no bus stations. When the conductor reached me, he was still speaking in Swahili, and I interpreted his inquiry as asking where we were going.

"Mombasa," I said.

Henry was so impressed that I could understand Swahili after only being in Kenya for a week. I think he thought my being Black and in Africa, I could intuitively understand the language. I believe Henry had this reaction because he was anxious being the only White person in the area, and had no experience in this environment. We arrived safe and sound at our resort in Mombasa around midnight. We were weary, but delighted that we had arrived safe and sound.

What I learned? Don't give in to your husband if he has a bad idea, no matter how much he insists, especially if his idea contains elements of danger.

Chapter

Forty-Three

Touring Africa made me reflect on race, and how racism might be different here in Kenya than in the United States. In the United States, being an interracial couple, made us stand out, this was not the case in Europe or in Africa. No one seemed to notice. As a Black person, living in the United States, racism was central to my existence, and to some extent being treated differently because of my color was the norm. I never thought about racism or discrimination affecting white people. One incident changed my perspective. In preparation for our move to Geneva, Henry and I, along with his Irish manager Dean, and his wife Mary, enrolled in a French immersion course at The French Institute in Nice, France. We were assigned housing by the institute. I was not happy with the shabby accommodations we were assigned, and asked Henry if we could move to another place.

This was August when most Europeans take vacations. Many of them came to Nice, so there was almost no housing available. The only place Henry could find was a luxurious apartment overlooking mountains, and the Mediterranean. This was available because a couple had recently purchased it, and the husband died before they took ownership. It was expensive, beautifully decorated, with marble floors, and a lovely back garden. I loved it. As soon as we moved in, we invited Henry's Irish Manager, Dean and his wife Mary to Sunday dinner. After oohing, and aahing, and marveling over how beautiful our place was, they then asked what happened to our first apartment. I told them it was just sitting there empty because we could not get a refund. They asked to see it.

Afterward they returned, they said, "That place is a palace compared to the dump they gave us. They only gave us that dump because we are Irish."

This caused me to laugh because this is exactly what Black people say in the United States. "They only gave us this dump because we are Black."

I am not sure at what point when I first felt the effect of racism, although I was always aware of the different races. There were White and Chinese people living on our block when I was small. Our grocers were Jewish and many of my teachers in junior high school as well as the students were White. My first glimpse came when I would see White classmates in town with their friends or relatives and they refused to speak to me, even when I spoke to them first even though we were friendly at school.

My first blatant exposure came many years ago, when I lived in England with George and I was working for the United States Navy. Soon after I started work, the Navy hosted a black tie dinner dance at one of the posh London hotels. Being one who loves to dress up—a carryover from my aunt Willie—and someone who loves to dance—a carryover from my mother, I invited three other Black couples to join us.

During the reception, George found the seating chart, and told us that we were seated at table twenty-eight. When dinner was announced, we went into the well-decorated dining room, looking for table twenty-eight. It was nowhere to be found. After searching for it for some time, we asked a waiter to help us. He came back and told us he found table twenty-eight under the stairwell. We found this odd because tables twenty-nine and thirty were visible. I asked to see the person who assigned the tables. I was told it was Ted Duffy (an alias) and someone found him for me. The first thing he said after I asked why our table was out of sequence was, "I am not prejudiced. I am from Oklahoma and a Black woman raised me."

I told him that who raised him was not my concern. I only wanted to know why table twenty-eight was out of sequence. Our conversation was circular for a few minutes. Finally, he told me he did not know why table twenty-eight was out of sequence and then he promised to give me the best table at the next Navy affair.

When I returned to work on Monday, I asked to speak to the naval commander. I relayed what had occurred at the dance to him and he said he would look into it. Later that day, he called to meet with me. Ted Duffy was also at the meeting. The story the naval commander gave was that the restaurant had moved the table because it was blocking them from passing through to serve food to the other tables. If you believe that, there is a bridge someone wants to sell you.

I experienced similar occurrences throughout my life—some incidences were visible and apparent, others were more covert. I never failed to challenge the overt actions of racism. I'm always speaking up, and requiring the person involved to defend their behavior. Some answers were quite comical, and all were questionable, but familiar.

Being married to Henry a white man in the United States we encountered many occasions where we attributed the person's behavior to be racist. Here are a few:

When I am in line ahead of Henry, and Henry has the tickets for both of us, the person collecting the tickets looks behind me, and failing to see a person of color, they prevent me from proceeding.

Henry and I were in a reception line greeting Digital's Board of Directors and their wives. When Henry greeted one of the wives by saying "Hello, this is my wife Claudette." She responded, "WIFE?" To her credit, she quickly recovered, saying, "Claudette forgive me, it's been a long day."

Henry and I were seated at a fundraiser with four white couples. The dinner was a buffet. Henry volunteered to get dinner for both of us. When he gave me my dinner he had forgotten to get bread, and went back to the buffet line to get rolls. One of the white women at the able was so offended that Henry was waiting on me, that she asked, "What is he, your slave?"

"No. He just loves me."

We had only one aggressive experienced. One evening we were walking down the street with another white couple, and a car drove by and threw a raw egg at us accompanied by a racial epithet.

What I learned? Every society seems to have an out-group that they discriminate against. In Ireland and England, it was the Catholic Irish that was the out-group. India had the untouchables—Africa, Japan, and South America, all have their own out groups. Whoever is at the top steps on people at the bottom, and used whatever means necessary to maintain their power, resources and assets. When it comes to race in the United States the more things change, the more they stay the same.

Chapter

Forty-Four

$\mathcal{S}$OON AFTER HENRY AND I returned to the United States from Europe, I was confronted with a new role—caring for an elderly parent. My father died suddenly and being an only child, it fell on me to care for my mother who was almost totally blind. After my father's sudden death, my mother had a series of health issues. Apart from having surgery on her eyes, she had vascular problems and all of her toes on one foot had been amputated, this was followed by a hysterectomy. Being her only caretaker required that I be available full time, so I resigned from Digital, to take care of her. Anyone who has performed this role will attest to how stressful it can be, especially if your parent is difficult.

Through all of this Henry was his supportive self. He would listen as I complained about my mother. I remember his putting his arms around me after I shared a particular hurtful story about my mother. My mother had been declared legally blind. When she was with us, I had to do everything for her as she pretended that she could not see. This confused me, and I would say to my girlfriends. "If my mother cannot see, how can she dress herself with all her clothes matching?" "They would offer all kinds of explanations, they never rang true for me. One particular day my mother was listening to her soap opera on the television. She was still smoking then. I happened to come into the room as she went up to the screen door, place her hand just at the right place to open the door, went outside on the patio, and commenced to look around at the trees, grass, and the sky.

I was shocked, hurt, and angry. I just felt betrayed. Like my mother had been pretending to be blind when all the time she could see. This brought back a remark a friend made when I told him the doctor said my mother had only 35% vision in one eye. He said, "That is a lot of sight." Well my mother just proved him right.

When I relayed all this to Henry, he said, "Don't worry about it. Your mother just wanted your attention." But it still hurt. And deepened my resented and mistrust of her.

She and I were both relieved when she completed her treatment and was well enough to move back into her own home. The young woman I hired to stay with my mother at night so my mother would not be home alone was not happy with her assignment. She told me that my mother insisted that she go to bed when my mother went to bed, and made other demands that were just as annoying.

Fortunately for me, a few years later, my son Garry divorced and moved in with my mother, becoming her caretaker. Surprisingly, they got along and enjoyed each other's company. What a blessing for me!

With Garry living with my mother, it freed me up to reenter the world of work. I started off as an organizational consultant and volunteered on boards of nonprofits that served the needs of women and children. At the same time, I was focusing on my relationship with Henry, and attempting to my resolve my childhood issues, especially issues that concerned my relationship with my mother.

One morning when my friend Alberta, called to chat and found me extremely agitated. She asked what was going on with me.

After some thought, I said, "It is because I had to pick my mother up to take her to a doctor's appointment."

This was the effect my mother still had on me, even though I was over forty. My friend, who was a psychologist, gave me a puppet to use as a prop to delve in and to get an understanding as to why my mother still had this effect on me. I used the puppet as she instructed, asking the puppet (my inner child) the question, "Why does my mother still have this impact on me?"

After using this process several times, the answer came from free-associating. What I discovered was that I was still carrying her negative messages to me just as I had done as a child—that I was somehow flawed and unlovable. After reflecting on this for some time, I spoke to my inner child and affirmed her, saying she was good, brave, and worthy of love as a child, and she is worthy of love as an adult— even if she didn't get it from her mother.

Alberta, the same friend who gave me the puppet to help me heal my inner child, was also the person who connected me to a resource that was instrumental in restoring a connection between me and Henry later on.

Returning from Europe, Henry and I found our relationship changed, and not for the better. I think Henry was angry that I moved back to the States and left him in Europe. Although he never admitted this. He just took issue with everything that came up, and we were constantly, fighting, bickering, and disagreeing over minor things. We tried talking about things but, the discussions never seemed to resolve anything. After a while, being in a negative and angry place became normal for us. I was considering ending the marriage. And then Alberta called and invited us to a picnic. I accepted her invitation and a miraculous thing happened.

We arrived at the picnic and I approached her to say hello, without any prompting, she began to tell me about a couples' counseling workshop that she and her husband had attended and how much it had helped their marriage. I immediately asked her a lot of questions. She described the process they used, and gave me the names or the workshop leaders. I called them the following Monday and I was happy to find that there was a workshop on the coming Saturday. Henry knew our marriage was in deep trouble and was happy that I had found something that might help our relationship get back on track, so I registered on the spot. Henry and I attended the two-day couples' counseling workshop that I credit for not only saving our marriage but giving us the tools to work through any future problems, and to keep our love vibrant.

The workshop was based on the book by Harville Hendrix, Ph.D., *Getting the Love You Want: A Guide for Couples.* Understanding what caused our problems and having the skills to work through them, is a gift that has continued to make our marriage thrive and make our marriage to shine.

It is our good fortune that Henry came from a loving and caring family, and even though he did not understand what set me of sometimes, what he learned in the workshop helped him to stay present while we worked through our arguments and confrontations. A lot of our problems stemmed from the anger, open wounds, and invisible scars that I brought from my childhood that left me emotionally damaged.

My parents were not attuned to my needs and I entered adulthood with open wounds and lots of anger. This is why attending the couples' workshop was perfect for me, and as my mate for Henry.

The following are some key areas that were covered and important to use during the two-day couples' workshop:

Exercises to capture the history of our families, our childhoods, and the early attraction of our meeting. We found the information on control and power particularly useful.

We had to practice on how to be heard, and listen to each other without defending ourselves. and to compliment each other. We wrote love letters and focused on what originally attracted us.

These were valuable lessons for me because I am impatient, don't listen, and interrupt often. A large part of this is that I have Attention Deficit Hyperactive Disorder (ADHD). An explanation, but not an excuse.

The exercises helped me stop always pointing out what is wrong, and being too critical and not complimentary enough to Henry.

I am not sure what was most important for Henry, but the following story will attest that he learned something. At the beginning of the workshop, we were told that we would not remember everything we learned, but it would be in our internal systems. This was true then, and it is still true today, twenty-five years later. Here is an example that shows how it stayed in our systems.

Some years after the couples' workshop, Henry had a business in China and he traveled there often. He came home from a trip to China just before Christmas. The morning after his return, he asked what we were going to do the next day. Being one who loves parties, I was happy to relate that we were going to a friend's brunch, another friend's open house, and then to another friend's Christmas party.

He responded angrily, "I am not going to do all of that."

My normal response from "my wounded child" would have been, "DON'T GO, I DON'T WANT YOU TO GO WITH ME ANYWAY." This is the way the wounded child would have lashed out when her mother didn't want to attend her Junior High School graduation, or wouldn't buy her a new dress for the occasion, and when she felt unwanted and unloved. But with the knowledge I gained from the relationship workshop on Getting The Love You Want, I knew I was not the wounded powerless child. And Henry was not my mother. So, instead of lashing out, I said, "Henry, after having been gone for two weeks, I would have thought you would want to do anything as long as you were doing it with me."

He melted and we went to all the parties and had a great time. We are still having a great time. Where there is conflict, anger, or disappointment we tune into our systems, and use the knowledge and techniques we learned in the relationship workshop to resolve any issue or conflict.

What I learned? To be open to new ideas, suggestions, and recommendations from people. Try them, they might work.

Chapter

Forty-Five

*I*N MY WORK WITH women whether coaching, consulting, or counseling, the question of how to find the right man always came up. This question when presented to me, was similar to a question I presented to my professional healers. Can you like someone you are envious of? I never received a satisfactory answer to my question. But I felt compelled to make an attempt to answer the question that my clients and friends constantly presented to me. "How to find the right man?"

I had my own theory, and after several discusses with Henry and some friends, I decided to design a research project, to test my theory, and hopefully arrive and some useful information to share with my friends and clients on how they can find the right man. It was not a very sophisticated project. Consisting only of a survey where I asked both men and women a series of questions. While I was involved in designing the questionnaire I reflected on my personal experiences, and those of my friends who had been successful in finding their partner to guide me in creating the questions for the survey. After I conducted face-to-face interviews with the participants. Both men and women. The research question was, *what did women need to do to get the right man?* The most interesting thing about the answers was that most of them were alike.

Although there is significant information in the marketplace on how both men and women can find the right mate, my survey only focused on women finding the right man. Here is a sample of some of the questions and answers from the survey:

Question: What are attributes that attract you to someone?

Answer: Fun person, likes sports, extroverted and outgoing. Good habits, intelligence, challenging, not boring, beauty.

Question: How did the relationship start?

Answer: We met at a party. She was tall, attractive, great smile, could dance, friendly, and cuddly. She could communicate about life and issues beyond work. This makes a person more attractive and interesting.

Question: What attracts a man to a woman?

Answer: Intelligence, self-assertiveness, holistic view of the world, beauty.

Question: Describe an ideal mate?

Answer: Positive force in the world, enthusiastic about life, allows lots of space. A bit provocative around issues she discusses.

Question: What is romantic love?

Answer: Gushy and heady feeling about the world. Everything is wonderful. Attitude is strong with positive feelings about the person.

Question: What can women do to attract men?

Answer: Dress well all the time. Be interested in issues. Stay tuned into the world. Save time for the man. Save baby and small talk for girlfriends. Talk worldly and about important things with men.

Question: What qualities do men desire in women?

Answer: To be ethical and honest, intelligent, attractive, not gorgeous, but attractive.

Question: What are some things women do wrong in trying to get a man?

Answer: Builds a picture in her head that is a fantasy, that will not be what is going on. Trying to put her scenario on the scene. It's a turn off. Trying to move the man too soon too fast. Introducing him to all her friends, showing him off, and parading the meat. I got my man what do you think of him?

Question: What are some elements of flirting?

Answer: Eye contact. Jousting over issues, on whatever the issue is. Telling funny stories, physical touching, letting the arm rest there. Make compliments to excess.

Question: What are some ways to get men interested in you?

Answer: Learn about his interest, and get in concert with his interest. If he likes sports, buy a couple of tickets to the game.

Question: What are some ways to keep his interest?

Answer: Do it again. Go to the place you first met. Same hotel, same restaurant. Do things without giving up yourself. Don't be false. Move toward a center point. Share joys.

Question: What can women do to make men fall for them?

Answer: Take care of yourself physically. Be intelligent about the world. Have more interests than yourself. Dress well. Wear good clothes.

Question: What are some mistakes women make?

Answer: Presuming that the relationship will continue. Take him for granted.

Question: What are some ways to manage a man?

Answer: Wrong presumption to start with. To make it work listen extremely carefully. Be sensitive to his desires. Be accommodating, but don't be a pushover. Once in a while don't be available and test his level of need for you.

Question: What destroys love?

Answer: Selfishness. Overbearing. Egocentric.

Question: What are some techniques to improve a relationship?

Answer: Travel together and talk. Recreate a starting over scene. Recreate the initial building of the relationship. There was magic before. Good if you can find it again.

Question: What are some ways to keep him interested after the relationship has matured?

Answer: Do something significantly different. Switch it up. Talk about future possibilities. Don't spend too much time in women's groups. Don't let women's groups take precedence over the relationship. More than two nights a week, block out time for him.

Question: What can keep the spark and excitement alive in the relationship?

Answer: Have a surprise weekend. Pack his clothes, pick him up at the office, and go do something that is a real surprise. Take him out to eat. Tell him you love him in a number of ways.

Question: What should women know about men?

Answer: They are interesting creatures. Early on their penis is in charge more than their brains. High sex drive until middle years. It is important they feel desired. Do risqué sexy things. Wear a negligee. Look sexy. Design a honeymoon all over again.

Question: What do you do when you're looking for a new relationship?

Answer: Review all of the characteristics you like in people you know. Build a model and advertise it. Tell your friends what you are looking for.

Question: What should women never do?

Answer: Don't sign him up for things before checking in with him. Don't assume you have control over him or his calendar. Don't crowd him. Don't introduce him as your lover before he does it. Don't treat him like a girlfriend. Treat him as a separate mate.

Question: What advice would you give women?

Answer: A man likes his work and career. They are very important to him. Don't make him choose between going to work or being with you. This will kill a relationship quick. Important to have this communication early. Sort out what his priorities are in life. Don't try to be too important too early. Remember you just showed up.

Question: What are men's view of women?

Answer: It runs from they are "like his mother" to "slut." Where they see you depends on how you present yourself. Act like a lady in public. Your mother or important women in your early life set a standard and basic imprint of the kind of women you want later on. Men like challenges, make sure you are not too available. Your man never finds you more attractive than when he sees you through another man's eyes.

Although there is significant information in the market place on how men can find the right woman, my work consisted only on women finding the right man. My survey yielded the following key points:

- You must go where the men are. Many women say they want to get a man, but spend most of their time with women or married couples. Single men are not usually in this social group. Places they might be: golf clubs, gyms, professional conferences, or with other single men.
- You must flirt. Flirting is not being sexually suggestive, but letting the person know you are interested in them. Laugh at their jokes, let your hand linger on his arm a little longer.
- Pay attention to what they say by asking questions. People like people who like them.
- Be good company by showing interest in what they like. Once you meet a man and there is mutual interest, don't begin the relationship by unloading all of your baggage. Don't get too close too soon. Keep some emotional distance.
- Set boundaries. A barrier they can't cross. Keep a part of yourself as yours that you don't share.

- Make yourself interesting by reading the papers and being up on current events. Know what is going on in the world. Have an opinion that you can support. Interesting people are also interested in others.
- If you want a date to turn into a relationship, don't have sex for at least five dates or thirty days. Sex often gets in the way of getting to know the person.
- Try to develop an interest in sports if you don't already have one. Someone said that every man wants his women to be his buddy, watch a game, and share a beer.
- Be positive, keep your problems to yourself.
- Don't rush the relationship or make the guy make a premature decision.
- Be confident. Confident women are very attractive.
- When starting a relationship there are some things to know. You have to teach men how to treat you, what you like, what you don't, and what is not acceptable.
- Tell him what you want. Be specific and concrete. Don't say, "I want you to be more romantic." Instead say, "I would like for you to bring me flowers every Thursday."
- Give him plenty of praise.
- Scold him when he is bad.
- Once in the relationship, give lots of sex.
- A man who loves and respects his mother is a man capable of loving and respecting you.

What I learned? Important information that women can use in their pursuit of finding the man they want.

Chapter

Forty-Six

$\mathcal{A}$FTER MORE THAN 13 years of marriage, Henry and I realized how much we could still learn and benefit from a conference on loving relationships. So we purchased Gary Smalley's tapes from his conference. We learned how to get the love you want from the couples workshop based on the book by Harville Hendrix. Gary Smalley told us how to keep the love you have.

Henry and I were willing students, and we dedicated our time to learn and embrace the conference teachings.

We learned the foundation of all healthy relationships is you must recognize and value your mate's differences, let them know they matter, and that they are important to you. Here I share some of the critical points he made in the conference that Henry and I make a conscious effort to incorporate in marriage.

We do things together, we share time and participate in the other interest. Henry is a pilot and loves planes, so I flew with him, and attended airshows. I am very social and love parties. Henry escorts me to the events even though he would prefer staying home and watching the Celtics. We both are aware that we bring how we were parented or treated as a child into our present relationships. We learned that most communication is nonverbal. And the importance of showing each other that they are number one. It is not easy, but we try to get over hurt and anger quickly.

What was new to us and what Gary's conference gave us is how men and women are so very different, and the importance of the word HONOR, to attach high value to your mate. We attempted to learn and to remember these important differences as explained by Gary Smalley. Women are different from men. And how men need to value these differences because women's qualities are awesome.

- Every cell in a woman's body is different from a man.
- Men are stronger physically, but women are stronger health-wise. More baby boys die before and after birth than baby girls.
- Men have nearly twice the amount of blood as women in their bodies, and more muscles. This makes men stronger. The testosterone that baby boys get when in the womb makes them physically stronger and more aggressive than girls.
- Men are left-brain dominant. They can only use one side of eighty percent of the brain at one time. This makes them more factual, more objective, colder, factual, with more of an urge to conquer most challenges. They don't have same sensitivity as women; don't feel the same the emotions or sympathy.
- Women are eighty percent lateral; they can use both sides of the brain at the same time. This makes women more alert to the whole picture and grasp things. Women feel more, have more sympathy, and can relate to others more.
- These differences cause problems in the typical home.
- Women give and have the ability to relate and feel more romantic. Ninety-nine percent of romantic books are bought by women. They have a built-in desire for closeness and relationships. They hunger for intimacy.
- Men express facts, women express emotions.
- Women are more verbal. The average man speaks 12,000 words per day, women 24,000 or more.

- This causes problems because women want to talk when men have used up their supply of words early at work.

Other differences—women's brains are wired differently. Often they have a hard time reading a map. It's harder for them to see spatial differences. This is why they will get upset if a mate is driving too close to the car ahead. A man sees he has a lot of room.

- Men are driven to find solutions; women are focused on feelings and empathy. The differences show when shopping—women want to browse, men want to hunt find what they want, and leave.

Men are different before marriage—he is hunting for a mate, when he wins her he is off to focusing on something else. He is left-brain dominant and his objective is to solve the problem.

- Women are personal—they relate to the whole and need to know the players or person to be interested in the game. Men compartmentalize. Women are like a body of water, flowing together. Men can separate who they are from their surroundings. Men identify with what they *do*.
- Women get their identities from who they are, women feel deeply. Men generalize, women detail. They remember every little thing that they felt deeply.
- Women have a desire for a good relationship, and they naturally understand and recognize a good relationship. This is why a woman will often say, "Can we talk about this" when a man thinks things are going well.
- Men should listen. *The better the relationship the longer men live.*

To illustrate the difference between men and women, here is a personal experience. My husband and I went to a dance. A very attractive couple was dancing. The woman was wearing a gorgeous long evening dress with a slit up the front. They were excellent dancers. And we all commented on the woman's beauty and her dancing ability. On the way home, Henry and I were discussing the evening and the couple who were the great dancers.

Suddenly, he asked, "What is the name of the movie actress we saw the other night?

"Meg," I said.

"No," he said. "The other one."

"Tara."

"Yes," he said.

I asked what Tara had to do with the lady we saw dancing tonight.

"I read somewhere she does not wear underwear," he said.

His answer took me for a loop. While the women were admiring her dancing ability and her beauty, Henry, and I would guess some other men, were thinking about what she was not wearing under the dress. This is an example of the difference between men and women. Men focus on sex. I heard that men think of sex every seven seconds or more.

What I learned? With men, It is all about sex.

Chapter

Forty-Seven

AFTER SO MANY YEARS seeking out teachers and books and conferences that would help me disentangle from my childhood and free my marriage from those tentacles, I began to realize that the whole process of helping people identify obstacles in their lives was of great interest to me. It was around this time that I began to consider studying to become a life coach.

Researching and discovering answers to questions that help people in their personal or professional life is of great interest to me. It is my passion. As a professional coach and consultant my clients are often puzzled because by what it takes to be successful in organizations is often not clear or apparent. Finding the correct answers is important and critical to one's career. One must know how to successfully maneuver through organizations, or the corporate world. Some groups experience more difficulty than others.

As a young professional, I made many mistakes that hindered my career. Most were caused by my not knowing the corporate culture, and the things that would get me into trouble. As an example, the importance of keeping your own counsel, not always saying what you think, and being open to feedback. I witnessed others making similar mistakes. It was mostly women and minorities, who exhibited behaviors that got them into trouble, and when they did, it was not easy for them to recover. It seemed white males somehow knew what to do and not to do. Minorities and women who were 90% of my client base, didn't.

As a life coach and a corporate consultant, I wanted to share both what I had learned through trial and error, and what I learned through my research. I needed to codify these critical concepts so it would be easy to pass them on to others. It was from this vantage point that I decided to do research and find the answer to the hidden keys to corporate success, and what it took for women and minorities to climb the corporate ladder. My research project focused on corporate savvy, understanding corporate culture, leadership, the advantage of a mentor, and value of networking.

My research focused on asking participants questions on what is meant by corporate savvy, or understanding corporate culture? Their answers: It is the ability to learn the unwritten rules, to locate the power base in an organization, to build alliances, to understand the corporate environment and culture on what gets rewarded and what get punished, and to understand how to get along with people.

When participants were asked what is meant by the word *leadership* and what leaders do, the answers were consistent: Leaders have a vision for the future. They can vividly imagine the steps necessary to reach a goal; they inspire, influence, and persuade people to join them in their vision. They have the ability to transfer the vision into a strategic plan to achieve the goal. They are strategic thinkers, decision makers, and they can see the big picture and deal with large chunks of information simultaneously. They set standards and expectations, and leave a legacy.

I conducted this research in the late 90s, but things are not too different now. At the time I conducted this project, all of the men interviewed who were corporate leaders had had mentors, and the women had not. Most of the women used a number of professional friends and colleagues in the role of mentors. My interview questions focused on the importance of having a mentor and what mentors do. The feedback: Mentors tell you what you need to know, they open doors for you, they sell you, they lay out a career map for you, and tell you how to get to the position that is your goal. They tell you where the roadblocks are and block for you downfield. They protect you and help you to identify your added value.

The last questions in my survey consisted of the value of and how to build an effective network.

Webster's New World Dictionary defines network as an arrangement of interconnected roads of individuals developing contacts or exchanging information to further a career. My research clients outlined how to build an effective network. They stated that there is work involved in networking. If you want to take your career to the next level, you have to make the effort to build relationships over time. Look for opportunities to meet people who may be of value to your career and establish relationships with them, join social groups and professional organizations. Remember networking is a sharing process, a two-way street. When you meet someone you deem important, don't try too hard. Relax and build a relationship by finding common ground before you bring up any issues. Listen at least half as much as you talk—ask questions and show interest. Explore ways you can be of assistance to them. Learn to leverage what *you* have to offer.

Look for six degrees of separation—where you grew up, attended college, or worked. Don't strive to impress and leave the meeting on a positive note. Follow through on the first meeting with a note, email, or telephone call. Stay in touch by extending invitations, cards, or notes from time to time.

What I learned? It is more important in your career to be liked than to be competent. People hire, promote, forgive, and protect people they like.

Chapter

Forty-Eight

$\mathscr{B}$Y THE TIME I completed the research project on "how to find the right man" I had spent years working on myself, on my relationship with Henry, and on my professional development. It was time to take my career to the next level. I accepted a position as President and Chief Executive Officer at Topf Center for Dance Education. This was the first time that I had total responsibility for an organization and for the salaries and benefits of its employees. It was a bit daunting, but it gave me an opportunity to put all my knowledge and experience in organization and management effectiveness into practice.

This was a continuum on my journey of self-fulfillment. To being all I can be personally, professionally, and spiritually. I had done a lot of work on healing and self-discovery. Taking the reins at Topf Center for Dance Education as President and Chief Executive Officer provided the opportunity for me to learn, grow, and overcome challenge as a professional.

The organization taught dance to more than 2,000 students a week in the Boston public schools as part of their academic curriculum. Its mission was to use dance to foster self-esteem, discipline, and improve academic performance in Boston's public school children.

Being President of Topf Center was the most challenging and fulfilling position I had held to date. And I owe a big debt of gratitude to Dorothy Terrell and her late husband, Al Brown for recommending me.

Not long into the job, I discovered we had a significant budget deficit. Our revenue derived from three sources: from our school contracts, from grants, from teaching dance classes in our studio, and from annual fundraisers.

After a staff meeting where I explained the problem to our staff, I proposed two solutions—we could either lay off some teachers, or we could all take a ten percent salary cut including myself. To the board's surprise, the staff agreed to take the ten percent reduction to our salaries. Knowing this would solve only part of the problem I designed a fundraising event that I thought would raise $150,000. I got a lot of pushback from the board of directors because I was told, up until this point they had only raised $13,000 at their fundraising events.

One board member who owned a public relations agency, supported my proposal saying it was a good idea, and she thought it could be successful. One might ask why I had the confidence to think we could raise $150,000 when the most the organization had raised was $13,000. The answer was my amazing network.

Our plan included developing a marketing campaign, recruiting friends with name recognition to join the Topf Center's board of directors, and recruiting friends with corporate relationships to serve as chairs for the gala. When my friends were approached and asked to serve in various capacities, they all said yes. I was fortunate to have a relationship with several television journalists, and they all agreed to donate their time and celebrity to serve as cause.

Susan Wornick of Channel 5 Television generously hosted the gala kick-off party at her beautiful home. There were more than eighty people in attendance, and we received a commitment from them that they all would serve on our gala committees and provide resources to help us reach our revenue goal.

The Topf Center for Dance Education's gala, celebrated "An Evening of Dancers in Black and White," with a list of 100 prominent members from the Boston community serving of its committee. There were some doubting Thomases among the board members. Their doubts were fostered by what they saw when they attended the gala committee meeting. Out of 100 members on the gala committee, not more than eight or nine would be at a meeting. This convinced the attending board members that the event would be a flop.

I was no way worried. I didn't expect my friends to attend gala committee meetings, but I knew that once they gave me their word that they would come through. The actual night of the gala, someone said some of the board members came expecting to see the event fail. They were in for a big surprise, for the gala was a spectacular event and we exceeded our $150,000 goal, raising $157,000, and we sold out the 400 tickets that were available.

Raising the money was great, but the evening was so much more than that. It was a culmination of teamwork, effort, faith and good fortunate. From Susan Wornick's kick-off party to how we received the beautiful decorations for the gala, to the performance of the dancers, it all worked. When we booked the venue at The Arts Center, Cyclorama, we had no idea of how we would decorate this large empty space. But faith stepped in. The Center had booked a large wedding for Saturday at noon. Our event was Friday night. The wedding event planner called and asked if we would allow them to decorate the venue on Thursday because they would not be able to do it in time Saturday morning for the wedding. Although we pretended for a moment that this would be an inconvenience, we knew it was a fortuitous gift and realized how lucky we were to be the recipients of these beautiful wedding decorations that would be there for our event,

When our guests arrived for our gala, they were stunned to see the ceilings and walls decorated in multicolor silks, gorgeous lanterns hanging the ceiling, and beautiful plants adorning the walls and around the room. This was only the beginning to the night of splendor. Liz

Walker of WBZ Television, and Karen Ward of Channel 5 Television were the Emcees, and did marvelous a job connecting and warming up the audience, as well as adding their celebrity and fame to the evening. It is difficult for me to describe the feeling in the room when the gorgeous men and women of all hues from Arthur Mitchell's Dance Theatre of Harlem performed for us. As a tribute, The "Evening of Dancers in Black & White" honored Arthur Mitchell and the Dance Theatre of Harlem. And they truly honored us with their spell binding dancing on point to the music of James Brown and Aretha Franklin. It was simply electrifying. Everyone jumped to their feet and applauded at the end of the show. My cousin Karen, who was at the next table from mine, gave me a big thumbs-up. This event set the bar for all our future galas.

My amazing network had come through. The evening was a smashing success, and the support we received from the media was outstanding. The gala was the topic of conversation in our community for weeks. And one guest was overheard telling a friend later, that he had missed the "event of the year."

Henry's comment to Bea, a girlfriend of mine, when she said I had done an outstanding job. "She is a genius, she is just a genius." Bea and I got a good laugh out of this.

I am happy to write that after the evening, all my friends became a part of the Topf Center for Dance Educations community, and was there and lent their support for our future galas. Susan Wornick of Channel 5 continued to give our gala kick-off parties at her lovely home, and Liz Walker of Channel 4 WBZ continued to be the gala emcee.

Our friends' and supporters' commitment to Topf Center's fundraising galas continued through 2005, and 2006. Jacques d'Amboise, founder of the National Dance Institute was our 2005 Honoree. The gala featured performances by special guest artists from the New York City Ballet, Dance Theatre of Harlem, and the Boston Ballet, with a special appearance by the Reverend Dr. Ray Hammond.

It was necessary in 2005 and 2006 to find a larger venue because the 2004 event had sold out. Fortunately, an advisory board member, Priscilla Douglas, persuaded Joe Spaulding, the president of the Wang Center, to donate the Shubert and Wang Theatres for our affair. These are two of Boston's most prestigious theatres. Arriving at the theatre and seeing the marquee lit up and blazing in lights saying, "Topf Center for Dance Education Celebrates an Evening of Dancers in Black and White," took our breath away.

The husband of our founder, Margie Topf, said to her, "Margie, you always wanted your name in lights."

The performance was followed with an elegant after-party in the Wang Center lobby. Guests said the feeling in the room extraordinary. We had produced another elegant and sensational evening that exceeded our expectations. We raised $202,000.

Building on our successes, we continued to raise the bar and set challenging fundraising goals. In 2006, we honored Tina Ramirez founder of Ballet Hispanico. We presented performances by special guest artists: from Ballet Hispanico; the Boston Ballet; the Rock School; Topf Center's Youth Professional Ensemble; and a special appearance by the Reverend Dr. Ray Hammond. We had another successful event where we raised $210,000.

The producer of our three outstanding galas was Richard Rien, a former dancer of the American Ballet. It was Richard's creativity, fabulous productions, and the generosity of our supporters that made the Topf Center for Dance Education a brand in three years.

What I learned? You can step out on faith if you have friends who have your back and won't let you fall.

Chapter

Forty-Nine

GIRLFRIENDS, GIRLFRIENDS, THE JEWELS in my crown. My girlfriends are precious to me for many, many, reasons. One, I am an only child with no siblings. I am told that your siblings are closer to you than your parents because they have been with you and shared the same experiences at the same time, and place, and from the same vantage point. In the absence of having siblings, my girlfriends have been wonderful substitutes. Not having a close emotional relationship with my mother made the emotional bonds that I formed with my girlfriends even more important and valuable. My girlfriends have played a critical role in my life since childhood beginning with my friendship with Meg.

Meg and I supported each other through very difficult times that I have already mentioned earlier in this book. Friendships between girlfriends is never one-way. There were many other occasions when my girlfriends and I were there for each other. Vera, a close friend and neighbor needed a dress to wear to a special affair. This was a last-minute invitation and she really wanted to go. So, I took one of my mother's best dresses, and lent it to her. She looked smashing, and had a marvelous time. Thank God, my mother never found out. This is what girlfriends do for each other.

When I was still in high school, our doorbell rang around 6 o'clock one evening. When I answered the door, I found my girlfriend Delores standing there in her beautiful yellow prom dress. I gave her money to pay the cab and escorted her into our living room. Through her tears she told me that the boy who was to take her to the prom had stood her up, and she didn't want her mother to know. So she left the house, hailed a cab and came to my house. I felt so sorry for her, and gave what comfort I could. But I knew the most important thing for her was that she had a girlfriend that she could depend on to be empathetic, comforting and discreet.

Girlfriends sometimes are there to save your life, literally. There have been two occasions when I intervened with my girlfriends who had life threatening illnesses and directed them to medical resources that they say save their lives.

On another occasion my girlfriend saved my husband, Henry's life. Henry was not feeling well one morning, but said he had to go to work to attend an important meeting, from noon to two o'clock, but, after the meeting, he would return home and go to bed. I left for Martha's Vineyard that morning to join friends for a few days. I called Henry that afternoon to see how he was felling, but he didn't answer. Thinking he must be sleeping, I called him again a few hours later. And then I called every hour after that. When I couldn't reach him, I became worried and called our children, but couldn't reach them either.

This was around seven o'clock and I had not reached Henry. I then called my girlfriend Sue. After I explained my concern, not being able to reach Henry, she said, "I am on it. I am leaving right now for your house, and calling my husband, Gordon, to meet me there."

I finally heard back from them an hour later. They told me that when Henry let them into them house, they asked him why he had not answered the phone. He told them he did not feel like talking. Gordon felt that Henry looked unwell and called his doctor, but when Sue recognized how sick Henry actually was, she called 911, and they sent an ambulance. The medical team said if Henry had not gotten antibiotics in the next 24 hours, his body would have gone into sepsis, and he would have died. There is no one like a girlfriend.

Most men don't understand the intimacy and trust women share. I remember having a conversation with my girlfriend's husband, James, who was boasting about his accomplishments, and his success in his field. He said he was especially proud because he was able to accomplish these things in spite of having had difficulties his early life. He didn't say what the difficulties were, only citing that some were very serious, juvenile offenses. He told me that he had kept his past a secret, and no one knew what had actually taken place except his wife, Gladys. My response to him was, "I would bet you money that your wife's best friend knows not only about the infractions, but every detail." He laughed in disbelief. What he didn't know, that most women tell their best friend everything.

Debra Haupert writes in her article about "The Girlfriend Instinct – The Value of Friendships," that women pull toward female friends as a primary support system in times of great stress. And the time spent with female friends tend to reduce stress levels. When women are with girlfriends their bodies emit the "feel good" hormone. She adds, women's self-esteem is highly influenced by girlfriends, and women without strong female social ties risk serious health issues.

These are some examples of when a woman calls a girlfriend:

Hear bad news, call a girlfriend. Have something to celebrate, call a girlfriend. Have a life changing diagnosis, call a girlfriend.

"Life is easier and better together with your girlfriends."

Many years ago, a friend emailed me this letter:

To all my girlfriends! I love you all! Young and newly married, I relaxed under a pecan tree on a hot, Texas summer day, drinking iced tea and getting to know my new sister-in-law, Estelle.

Not much older than I, but already the mother of three, Estelle seemed to me experienced and wise.

"Get yourself some girlfriends," she advised, clinking the ice cubes in her glass. "You are going to need girlfriends. Go places with them; do things with them."

What a funny piece of advice, I thought. Hadn't I just gotten married? Hadn't I just joined the couple-world? I was a married woman, for goodness' sake, not a young girl who needed girlfriends.

But I listened to this new sister-in-law—I got myself some girlfriends. As the years tumbled by, one after another, gradually I came to understand that Estelle knew what she was talking about. I remembered that she had said the word "girlfriends" with emphasis. As I went along, I discovered the subtle difference between friends and girlfriends. You go to work with friends, go to dinner with friends, go to church with friends, belong to clubs with friends. You send friends greeting cards. You need friends in your life; all girlfriends were once only friends. But a girlfriend is different. I offer this praise of girlfriends. Here is what I know about girlfriends:

- ✓ Girlfriends don't compete.
- ✓ Girlfriends bring casseroles and scrub your bathroom when you are sick.
- ✓ Girlfriends keep your children and keep your secrets.
- ✓ Girlfriends give advice when you ask for it—sometimes you take it, sometimes you don't.
- ✓ Girlfriends don't always tell you that you're right, but they're always honest.
- ✓ Girlfriends still love you, even when they don't agree with your choices.
- ✓ Girlfriends might send you a birthday card, but they might not. It does not matter in the least.
- ✓ Girlfriends laugh with you, and you don't need canned jokes to start the laughter.

✓ Girlfriends pull you out of jams.

✓ Girlfriends don't keep a calendar that lets them know who hosted the other last.

✓ Girlfriends will give a party for your son or daughter when they get married or have a baby, in whichever order that comes!

✓ Girlfriends are there for you, in an instant and truly, when the hard times come.

✓ Girlfriends listen when you lose a job or a husband.

✓ Girlfriends listen when your children break your heart.

✓ Girlfriends listen when your parents' minds and bodies fail.

My girlfriends bless my life. Once we were young, with no idea of the incredible joys or the incredible sorrows that lie ahead. Nor did we know how much we would need each other. I want to tell women to take my sister-in-law's advice. Get yourself some girlfriends. You are going to need them.

This next story reflects the sentiment and the important role that my girlfriends have played in my life. I remember one particular instance, as part of my husband's alimony agreement he had to carry a very large life insurance policy, with his ex-wife as beneficiary. After retiring from Digital, at his advanced age, this large amount was extremely expensive to purchase on the open market. Because he was busy working, I offered to help find an affordable option. After searching for many days and long hours on the telephone with insurance agents, I found an insurance company that offered the coverage at half the price of what had been quoted by others. I was so pleased and excited when my Henry came home, I blurted out that I had found life insurance with the needed coverage at half the price that had been quoted by other insurance companies.

His response was, "You are trying to cheat my ex-wife."

Stunned by his response, I immediately dialed my girlfriend in New York. When she answered the phone, I started balling. She was alarmed and asked what was wrong.

I said, "I am married to a fool."

Girlfriends understand, they are there to hear us, console us, and cheer us.

Because our girlfriends are so important to us we expect too much from them. Much more than we expect from our husbands or children. When we fight with our family members, we quickly get over it, even if they had done some mean or egregious We forgive them. But let a girlfriend let us down, or fail to live up to some imaginary ideal of a friend, our anger and sense of betrayal runs deep and every lasting. There have been months when some of my closest and dearest friends, did not speak or talk to each other. Trust me, if I cited them here, which I won't for privacy, you would say "what, that kept you from speaking for four month or three years?" The demands we place we on our girlfriends can be unreasonable: that they will always be the perfect friend, never disappointing us, and are always there when we need them. It would be hard for anyone to measure up. But sometimes this is what we expect when we choose a person and give them the title of girlfriend.

For me girlfriend is a special word. It signifies trust. I have often stepped out on faith because I knew my girlfriends would be there to support me. A great example is when I was the president and CEO of the Topf Center for Dance Education and committed to raising $150,000 after only being in the job for two months. I was confident in making this claim because of my girlfriends. I knew they would have my back. Another time I designed a girls' mentoring project for the college bound students at Wheelock College. We needed thirty mentors for the thirty students. My girlfriends stepped up and volunteered. At our orientation on the first Saturday morning, one friend, Kimmie, said she hated me that morning because she had to take the red eye from Los Angeles to make our morning meeting. This is what girlfriends do, you can count on your girlfriends.

The girls in the program were so impressed with the women, because they had never interacted with successful women who they could use as role models. We ended the program that summer by taking the mentees to Martha's Vineyard. Again, my girlfriends gave their support and hosted the mentees in their homes. Most of the girls had never been to Martha's Vineyard and some had never been on a boat. This was a great display of friendship and we all had a splendid time. Here is a letter that I received recently from one of the parents:

> *Good Morning Ms. Crouse,*
>
> *You won't remember me; but I remember your group participated in a mentorship program at Wheelock College Upward Bound Program. At that time my daughter Jazmyn Smart was in the program. You and others sponsored a trip for the young ladies to Martha's Vineyard. I wanted to share that Jazmyn graduated from Rhode Island College on Saturday and has been accepted to Babson College where she will pursue her Masters of Science in Accounting in preparation to sit for the CPA Exam.*
>
> *It's always nice to look back and appreciate those who had a role in shaping young people. It takes a village to raise our children and I wanted to say thank you and to keep inspiring the young women of our community.*
>
> *Best regards,*
>
> *Lisa Francis*

My girlfriends and I keep in touch by sending loving and inspiring emails, quotes, or prayers. I read them during quiet moments or when I need a spiritual lift.

- Girlfriends always offer support, sometimes literally. For example, my friend Anne sent me a gadget to exercise my facial muscles so they wouldn't sag.
- When my mother was in the hospital, they went with me to visit her.
- When my father died suddenly, they took over and made all of the arrangements.
- They prayed for me to become a Christian. I don't attend services on a regular basis, but still feel it is my spiritual home.
- During the part of the service where guests were invited to join the church, I was standing between my girlfriends Dorothy and Carol. They walked and stood with me while I committed to becoming a member of the church.
- They prayed with me in times of trouble, and walked with me to join the church.
- They held me when Reverend Gloria baptized me in Barnstable Bay.

What I loved most about Reverend Gloria was that she recognized I was ready to become a Christian. Thank God she did because I needed my faith to sustain me through many of life's challenges. Soon after I was baptized, my husband Henry was showing signs of cognitive impairment and I was deeply troubled thinking it might be Alzheimer's—which had killed his mother years earlier. Fortunately, his condition turned out to be only temporary.

I can remember reading the Bible as a young child, about eight or nine years old, and being touched by the messages of Jesus that seemed so hopeful and wise. The first was, "Don't worry about yesterday, it is gone, begin today and complete what you failed to do yesterday."

The other was his message in response to the Pharisees, who said one should not work on the Sabbath.

"If your lamb fell in the well on the Sabbath," he said. "Would you rescue it or would you let it drown?"

Of course if you rescued it, you would be working on the Sabbath. I fell in love with Him at this young age, even though I did not experience him as the Son of God at that time, only as a wise prophet.

Somewhere along the way, I embraced a philosophy and a practice of always wanting to leave more behind than was there when I came. As I got older and suffered with depression, I found that it helped my state of mind if I did something kind for someone. I think I was predisposed to becoming a Christian and I am eternally grateful to my Bible study sisters and Reverend, Dr. Gloria White Hammond. I count them all as girlfriends for providing me with the spiritual education on which my faith stands.

My girlfriends bring joy, light, and beauty to my existence. They have provided the love, support, and acceptance that I never received from my mother. I feel secure knowing they are there and I carry them in my heart.

What I learned? If you find yourself alone, late at night frightened because you are in the wrong place with the wrong guy, your girlfriend is only a call away.

Chapter

Fifty

I DIDN'T GROW UP IN a religious home. When I was a child my parents never went to church, and I was never baptized into any faith, although my grandparents were all Baptist. I member going to church with my maternal grandmother, Toolie, when I was very small child. It was a funeral and everyone was crying, and there were lots of flowers. For years, I associated flowers with death and sadness, and maintained a dislike for flowers for years, although the reason remained a mystery to me until I made the connection through therapy.

Although religion was not a part of my home life, I was often invited to attend church with some of our neighbors. Through these occurrences, I came to know about God, and about Jesus. And this exposure to religion and faith gave me some assurance that someone was watching over me. I now know that this was the bedrock to my ability to maintain some hope beneath all of the sadness that I experienced as a child.

At the age of nine or ten I started to read the bible and fell in love with Jesus; not as the Son of God, but as a wonderful and wise prophet. Three of Jesus' teaching stood out for me: don't worry about tomorrow; tomorrow is gone, deal with today. This has been one of my cornerstones for how I deal with adversity. or missed opportunities. When I tried to stop smoking, or to lose weight, or overcome other challenges, I think of this teaching, and say to myself, "Today is a new day to do what I was unable to do yesterday."

The second teaching that stood out for me was the saying of not to work on the Sabbath, the Sabbath should be kept holy. Jesus said, "If you had a lamb and it fell in the well on the Sabbath, would you let your lamb drown, or would you rescue it? If you rescue, you are working on the Sabbath." I think this was his criticism to the Pharisees who were very legalistic, but not too holy. This has been helpful to me in trying to distinguish between the rules I should follow and the rules I should ignore. This fostered a sense of independence in me. Not to be obedient automatically. To always question authority.

The third lesson that I have use as a guide for my life is the lesson you reap what you sow. It has been one of my driving principals. To always be aware that what I do has consequences, and that my behaviors will serve me well, or they will serve me ill. In this regard, I have always tried to leave behind more than what was there when I came.

When I attended church I did not particularly enjoy church. The messages I heard were all about sin and damnation, and you had to die to go to heaven and be happy. My childish thoughts were, later for heaven if you have to die and go there to be happy. So my faith in religion was slow in developing. And took decades before I made a commitment to practice a particular religion.

My spiritual quest was ignited when I read the book the *Road Less Travelled* by Scott Peck. This is a spiritual self-help book, and the title *The Road Less Travelled* lets us know that the road to spiritual grown and development is not easily taken. It takes a lot of strength, discipline and courage to accept responsibility for our own personal growth. His premise is life is difficult, and we have to overcome our problems through suffering, discipline and hard work. The ability to postpone gratification is a key component of our spiritual development. Dr. Peck provides tools to guide us to a New Psychology of love, traditional value and, spiritual growth.

After embarking of this new pursuit of spiritual growth, my friends and I read and attended lectures on various related subjects. During

Lent one year, we attended a lecture by Harold S. Kusner, author of *When Bad Things Happen to Good People*. He wrote this book for people who were believers, but had experienced tragedies that might have them question God.

Rabbi Kushner's message was that bad things happened to everyone, including good people. He said it is important to teach our children to make room in their life for pain so, when it comes they don't turn to drugs, alcohol, sex, gambling, or other destructive behaviors ways to avoid feeling the pain.

These two books connected with me both psychologically and spiritually, and caused me to reflect and question my internal self as well as what role I wanted spirituality to play in my life. So, when my friend Anne introduced me to Buddhism, I was already open to joining and participating in an organized religion. Up until this point, I had never been a member of any organized religion.

I joined the Buddhist group with my friend Anne, and immediately felt the positive benefits of my practice. This was right after my father's sudden death from a stroke, and I was still grieving and feeling guilty that I should have been able to save him. Clearly, this was irrational thought. Anne and I attended Buddhist meeting weekly, and someone spoke at each meeting on how the practice had impacted their life. When it came time for me to tell my story, on how Buddhism had changed my life, I talked about how it had given me confidence that I could make my life whatever I chose, it all depended on me; on what I thought, on what I felt, and on what I did. It was all based on the law of Karma, you got back what you send out. This is exactly the message I had gotten from Jesus so many years ago when I was reading the bible. "You reap what you sow." This was profound. It gave the person some control. If they wanted good things, they did good things. During my twelve years practicing Buddhism, I prayed and meditated on the prayer of St. Francis of Assisi. This prayer had a deep and profound impact on my spiritual development and prepared me for the transition from Buddhism to Christianity.

I always say God came and got me. And I came to Christianity by default. When my Buddhist sisters, Anne and Betty, moved to Washington, D.C., I was spiritually lonely. My friend Liz had recently recommitted to her faith and joined Bethel AME church. I suggested to her that we form a spiritual group. She said I suggested we form a bible study group. In any case, she and I invited eight friends to a meeting and her pastor, Reverend Dr. Gloria Hammond, came to guide us in our study. Since I was a Buddhist, my expectations were that we would study and converse on all religions. But everyone at the meeting was a Christian and had no interest in discussing or learning about Buddhism.

At our first meeting, I started to ask questions about Christianity, and was given a Life Application bible that was written in layman's terms. After asking several people what being a Christian meant, and not being satisfied with their answers, I read through the bible, placing post-it notes at places that gave me what I thought was a good explanation. By our next meeting, I had my answer. Being a Christian means loving God, loving you, and loving others. Being a Christian means love.

Shortly after I joined the Bible study group, a friend in New York sent me a book that she found in her boyfriend's library. It was on the nature of religion, and explained the Good News, and stated why Christianity transcended Buddhism. This gave me a clearer understanding of Christianity and I thought about becoming a Christian. The benefit would be that I would not have to pay the Karmic debt. (*Smile*)

After meeting for a year, we had a retreat at a friend's home in Barnstable, MA. When I arrived at the retreat the only available seat was next to Reverend Gloria our Bible study leader. I thought this was divine providence because I had planned to ask her to baptize me.

"Reverend, Gloria," I asked, sitting next to her. "I want you to baptize me, but I don't want to necessarily become a member of your church because I have not visited other churches. Is that a problem?"

She asked why I wanted to be baptized. I told her that I had been on this spiritual journey for over fifteen years, that I had been a practicing Buddhist for over twelve years, and that Buddhism had taught me to love myself, warts and all, but Christianity had taught me to love everyone. And to love and forgive everyone is very freeing and liberating.

After hearing my response, she asked if I wanted to be baptized right then.

"Can we?" I asked, not knowing this would be the cause of an uproar with some of my Christian sisters. I since learned that usually there was a requirement of study before one could be baptized. But a strong voice, Reverend Gloria's, in the group prevailed and it was agreed that Reverend Gloria would go forward with baptizing me.

So off we all went to Barnstable Bay, and I was baptized in the ocean at sunset, with Kathy and Fran holding me, and Reverend Gloria baptizing me. She read the sermon about the Eunuch who was on the road from Damascus and on hearing about Jesus, asked to be baptized. Although our bible study group no longer meet, there is still a spiritual connection, that bonds us.

Buddhism taught me to love myself warts and all, and Christianity taught me to love everyone warts and all. When you love everyone your heart is light, because it is a heart full of love, mercy, and forgiveness.

I feel so grateful, and know that I have been truly blessed, as I access my life, that I have learned to love and accept myself, learned to love and accept my mother, have had a successful and satisfying career, found true love with Henry, and formed a deep and abounding connection with God.

Postscript

$\mathcal{I}$ BEGAN THIS BOOK BY telling my readers about my unhappy childhood, and how poorly my parents treated me. But, sometimes in life things come full circle. My father died suddenly in 1987 and left enough funds to provide for my mother until she died 25 years later. She would always say my father was a good provider.

He not only took care of my mother, he took care of our whole family. After he died, my son Garry said, "Mom, Grandpop always took care of us, and he is still taking care of us." The money he left me came at a time when I most needed it. And I thank him.

I also give thanks to God that my mother lived long enough for me to make peace, and forgive and love her. The origin of forgiveness started when an older woman in one of my psychology classes at Harvard made the remark, "...when I gave up the myth of childhood."

I asked her, "Mary, what is the myth of childhood?"

She answered, "It's when you think your parents are just your parents, and don't realize that they have many other roles to play in their lives, and that they also had parents."

I had an epiphany one day that if I were going to blame my mother for the things that are wrong with me, I had to give her credit for the things that are right with me and there is much more right than wrong.

The time for fully forgiving my mother came a day before her death at the age of 89. She was in the hospital and there was no circulation in her right leg. The doctors wanted to amputate it. She rejected the operation because she didn't want to be dependent on anyone, living with just one leg. Her surgeon told her she would die from gangrene without the surgery. She told the doctors she had enjoyed her life—raised a daughter, two grandsons, and had a beautiful great granddaughter, and they were all doing well. Plus, she said jokingly, "I can't have sex anymore, so I am ready to go."

She asked me what I thought. I told her it was her decision and I supported whatever she chose. Every day we checked in with her to see if she had changed her mind. I asked her if she was afraid to die.

She said, "It is what I have to do, so what is there to be frightened of?"

My mother lasted two more weeks. The day before she died I felt this strong urge to see her and tell her all the things she had given me. I wrote down a list and read it off to her.

She said, "It was all in a mother's love."

"I still appreciate it," I said.

My son Garry came, and I told my mother I was going outside to speak with him. Before I left, I went to kiss her, and said, "You are a tough old broad."

She knew that this expression contained how proud I was of her courage. She looked up at me with the brightest and biggest smile, and asked, "Do you like me?"

I said, "Yes."

This last encounter was her gift to me, and I will cherish it all the days of my life.

She died the next day. My son George was with her when she started transitioning. She called her mother's and her sister's names. And George asked her, "Grandmom, can you see them?" She didn't answer and died shortly after.

My mother had a beautiful funeral service and celebration of her life. My sons, stepsons, and step-grandson were the pallbearers. The minister was connected to my sons' father and did a great job. I spoke about the benefits of living a long life—one being you get a greater perspective on appreciation, gratitude, and forgiveness.

I experienced all of these in my mother's and my case. At the service, I talked about what I appreciated about my mother: her strengths, her talents, her generosity, her sense of humor, grace and courage. Even when challenged with the sudden loss of her husband, with the loss of her sight, and the necessity of going on dialysis, she never once complained.

I spoke of our last visit, and how alert she was mentally, giving me the names of people from our distant past. Her spirit and humor never wavered. She had no fear. I thanked her for all the gifts she had given me. When she said it was all in a mother's love, I said I want to thank you anyway.

When I looked over the congregation at the funeral I saw the many young people my mother had taken in. Just like she did when I was a child and we lived in Philadelphia. Our house was the place friends and relatives came to live when they had fallen out with their parents, friends or spouses. My mother provided a place for them. Now they were here with their spouses and children, and spoke with love and humor of how it was living with my mother. There were at least 10 there who had lived with my mother over the twenty-five years she had lived in Nashua. They all spoke of their appreciation, and my mother's toughness. And how she taught them all to cook collard greens.

We returned to my house for food, drinks, and more stories.

A perfect ending to a good life.

What I learned? When we cling to the negative or the unjust in our past, we unwittingly bring it into the present, and though we don't realize it, we force the people in our lives to accommodate the old patterns – even sometimes reenact them with us. Eventually the negative from the past becomes a destructive factor in the present. When we learn this, then we truly see that turning the other cheek or offering forgiveness isn't simply behavior we emulate by virtue of its moral superiority, or a sacrifice of some kind. It is instead an act of supreme compassion. Its like cutting away a tangle of netting and rope from a dolphin so it can move the way it's supposed to. We realized that the first half of the prayer of St. Francis (Where there is hatred, let me sow love, where there is injury, pardon; where there is doubt, faith, where there is despair, hope; where there is darkness, light; where there is sadness, joy.) isn't a tall order asking us to be stoic and selfless – instead it's saying this is kind of the magic formula to bring these wonderful things into our own lives, for us, because St. Francis means it literally when he says, "For it Is in giving that we receive, it is in pardoning that we are pardoned, it is in dying, (to the self – the ego) that we are born again to eternal life."

When I learned to forgive what was done in my parents marriage, and when I was able to compassionately care for my mother even though she had been unkind to me, it cleared away the obstacles in my marriage, and in my relationship with my own children.

When I forgave my mother, my sons, George and Garry, forgave me.

GOD IS GREAT!!!!!!!

Epilogue

$\mathcal{B}$EFORE I EMBARK ON the next phase of my life's journey, I want to share the three important lessons I learned about faith, gratitude and perseverance while completing this book.

When I started writing this book over four years ago, my life was on an even keel. My husband, Henry and I had no apparent health issues; our finances were sound, being managed by a competent financial advisor, and Henry was president of an early stage company. Then everything came crashing down. Henry was diagnosed with a very serious illness, our finances plummeted through the lack of his oversight, and he was abruptly removed from his position without compensation. I felt like Job in the Bible with everything coming at once: Henry's illness, having to sell our home on Martha's Vineyard, and having to hire lawyers to negotiate a fair financial severance package from Henry's company. If you have had experiences dealing with lawyers, you know this can be stressful in and of itself. Before there was a settlement we had hired three different lawyers, and things only got resolved when a dear friend put his reputation on the line and pressured Henry's company to settle. He was not a lawyer.

The daily stress and pressure on me having to deal with these issues became so intense that one afternoon it reached its peak and I couldn't see. My eyesight became so fuzzy and images ran as in a movie reel. I called my neighbor, Gordon, to take me to the hospital, but he told me

199

to call an ambulance because they would triage me on site. I refused this route because I didn't want the drama. He called the ambulance himself and went with me to the emergency room. The doctors all feared I was having a stroke, but that fortunately, wasn't the case. After many scans, MRI's and other exams, they finally determined that I had suffered an internal migraine.

Faith

These were very challenging times. And everything fell on me due to Henry's being ill. I had to learn to manage things I never thought I was capable of doing: dealing with financial institutions, making decisions about Henry's treatment, negotiating legal contracts, selling assets. During all of this I was not sure if my decisions were the best. It was during this time that I learned the power of faith. When there is nowhere else to turn, if we have faith, we can turn to God. Every morning I prayed, asking for God's mercy and help during this dark time in our lives. And then I would randomly open the Bible and read a passage on the page that appeared, absorbing the spiritual message for comfort and support. One particular morning when I was in total despair, the passage I randomly turned to was Matthew 14:26 where Jesus said, "Why are you afraid, don't you trust Me? It is all right, I am here! Don't be afraid." This passage, on that morning, was exactly what I needed to affirm: that God was with me and I could trust Him to see me through these trials and tribulations.

Another passage that got me through a very tough day was Psalms 121:1-2, "I will lift up mine eyes unto the hills, from whence cometh my help. My help cometh from the Lord, which made heaven and earth." It was the power of faith that sustained me through my darkest days and scariest times. And believe me, those times were dark and scary. I learned that faith is like a muscle, the more you exercise it the stronger it gets.

A strong muscle will support your body; a deep faith will support your life. Someone once asked Debbie, a friend of mine, "Debbie, why do you pray?" Her answer, "Because it works."

Here is a story about faith that I heard many years ago while viewing a religious program on television. The exchange was between a priest and a young medical resident.

"Father you are always talking about God. Where is He, I can't see Him? I don't believe He exists." The priest asked the young medical resident. "Have you ever dissected the brain?" "Yes father, he answered." "Did you see any thoughts there?" "No father." "Did you ever dissect the eyes?" "Yes father." "Did you see any sight there?" "No father." "Did you ever dissect the heart?" "Yes father." "Did you see any love there?" "No father." The priest continued, "You did not see thoughts, you did not see sight, you did not see love, but you know they are there."

This is the answer I give to my family and friends who question my belief in the existence of God.

Gratitude

The next important lesson I learned is the importance of the gift of gratitude. Someone once said there can be no happiness without gratitude. There are many people who seem to have so much: health, wealth, beauty, and fame, but they are seemingly joyless and are frequently chronic complainers. They are not thankful for their gifts. They take them for granted and tend to focus on what is missing rather than on what they have.

When I was a young professional working at a digital equipment plant, a friend commented about the difference between Jeanette, another colleague (not her real name), and me. He said, "Claudette, you and Jeanette are both spoiled, but there is a difference in the two of you. When you get your way and what you want, you are thankful, but

Jeanette's attitude is, "Why didn't you give it to me yesterday?" He was highlighting an example of ingratitude.

My gratitude grew stronger when, one day, I had an epiphany during a Bible study class. We were talking about the darkest night sometimes comes before the dawn. All of a sudden, I realized that my mother was blind and could not see the dawn. And what a wonderful blessing and gift it is to be able to see. Every day since that time, I wake up with joy and a great sense of gratitude for all the gifts I have, which like most people have, are many. If you want to develop gratitude, just look around and see how so many people are dealing with extremely challenging life issues: physical, mental, financial, or worst. To the extent you are fortunate to have a life that is free of these troubles, you can be grateful.

I am very grateful that Henry's surgery was successful. He has recovered, a friend negotiated a lucrative settlement from his former employer, and he is working as an advisor in a company he loves. My gratitude extends to a dear friend that cared enough to involve himself in Henry's dispute and used his power and influence to arrive at a successful outcome.

Perseverance

Another lesson I learned is the importance of perseverance. After my life settled back into a normal rhythm, I tried to return to writing and completing this book. But I had lost the connection to my manuscript. No matter how hard I tried to continue on the subject at hand, I drew a blank. After struggling for more than a month without making any real progress, the thought came to me to, "Just write. You only have to write one sentence or one page at a time, but write. The important thing is to get started."

So every morning for a few months, I got up, went to my computer and just wrote whatever came to mind. I titled these writings by date. Doing these extemporaneous writing exercises paid off, and finally triggered some thoughts and ideas that were connected to my manuscript. This taught me the importance of moving forward and taking the next step; that doing something, even if it wasn't directly on point, was better than doing nothing. This was a strategy that I adopted and used in all kinds of ways: in completing this book, in exercising, or doing tasks that I found long and arduous. I would say to myself, "Just do a part. Doing something is better than doing nothing. Begin the task, take the first step, and keep moving forward." I found this particularly useful when I tried to stop smoking. Sometimes I would go days or weeks without smoking and then I would relapse. I came to understand that I did not develop the habit of smoking overnight. It took some time before I became addicted, and it might take time for me to break the addiction. So I told myself to, "Just keep trying every day, every week, every month, until you build a new habit of not smoking. There is a Buddhist saying, "The journey of a thousand miles begins with the first step." Many times success is predicated on taking small continuous steps, or taking life in small bites.

I pray in gratitude for all my blessings every morning. Being alive is the greatest blessing, and I am also grateful that I have the ability to love.

The lessons I learned about Faith, Gratitude, and Perseverance have brought me to this place—a place of peace, joy, and love. I wish the same for all my readers.

PHOTO GALLERY

Top Photo: Claudette Crouse on Paradise Island
Bottom Photo: Claudette Hodges Pendleton
Crouse's high school graduation photo

Top photo: Ella Hodges - Claudette's mother
Bottom photo: Claude Hodges - Claudette's father

*Top photo: Annabelle Lowery - Claudette's
maternal grandmother, and Claudette
Bottom photo: Willie Dunaway, Claudette's aunt and mentor*

Top photo: Howard Dunaway- Claudette's cousin
Bottom photo: Fannie and Howard Dunaway

*Top photo left to right: Thelma Bagget, Clarence Dempsey, George
Pendleton, Claudette's first husband and Claudette
Bottom photo: Claudette and George Pendleton at a formal in London, England*

Top photo: Claudette in her home in Fairbanks, Alaska
Bottom photo: Alexandria Traylor, George's granddaughter in front
of his former home in Harold On The Hill in London, England

Top left photo: George and Garry Pendleton in Rimini, Italy
Top right photo: Garry playing ball in Florida
Middle left: Garry and George with friends
Middle right: Garry and George with aunts Seal and Del in Tampa, Florida
Bottom left: George and Garry in St. Marks Square
Bottom right: George and Garry in St. Peter's Square

Claudette Crouse graduating from Harvard
University, Renee Bridges behind her

Top left photo: George and Garry with friends in Italy
Top right photo: Garry and George playing in
their backyard on Cunningham Park
Middle photos: Claudette's classmates, Joe and Kitty
Palermino with Henry and Claudette's
Bottom left photo: Claudette and Garry, as Garry leaves for prep school
Bottom right photo: Claudette with classmates at graduation, including
Shiela Azores. Renee Bridges with Colby hiding behind program

Claudette and Henry Crouse's wedding photo

Top photo: Claude, Claudette and Ella Hodges - Claudette's parents
Bottom photo: Charles and Renee Bridges, with Claudette at her wedding

216

Top photo: Henry, Claudette and Bennie and Flash Wiley at Crouse wedding
Bottom photo: David Fields, Henry Claudette and
Marian Taylor, Crouse wedding party

217

Top left photo: Claudette, Karen Hodges, and Patrina Calwell
Top right photo: Henry and Claudette in Venice
Middle photo: George Pendleton and Alane Ciriello
Bottom photo: Henry and Jo-Ann Sheehan

Top photo: Claudette and Henry in the Bahamas
Bottom photo: Claudette with her mother Ella Hodges at Lake Tahoe

Top photo: Claudette and Renee and Claudette and Henry cutting wedding cake
Bottom photo: Claudette and Henry in Kenya

Top photo: Claudette and Henry on cruise
Bottom photo: Henry and Claudette at a party

Top photo: Garry and his mother. Claudette in the Bahamas
Bottom photo: George and his mother, Claudette in the Bahamas

Top photo left: Harold Jara and Julia Pendleton
Top right: Friends at Crouse party
Middle left: Joe, Charles, Renee and Kitty at Crouse going
away party on their move to Geneva, Switzerland
Middle right photo: Bob Glover helping Liz Walker
as they leave Crouse New Year's Eve party
Bottom left: Julius Hodges, Claudette's uncle, Claudette
with friend Helen and her husband
Bottom right: George Searles celebrating Claudette's college graduation

Top photo: Claudette with granddaughter Julia Pendleton
Bottom photo: grandson Arrik Crouse

Top photo: grandchildren Julia and Arrik
Bottom photo: son and daughter, Richard,
and Linda Crouse with father Henry

Top photo: Arrik Crouse at Boy Scout meeting
Bottom photo: Arrik fishing

Top photo: Cousin Karen Walker with daughters Rachael and Olivia
Bottom photo: granddaughter Julia with friend Molly on Martha's Vineyard

Top photo: Granddaughter Julia and grandson Jordan Jara
Bottom photo: grandchildren Julia, Jordan and Youssef Sidi

Top photo: Julia's high school graduation
Bottom photo: Julia, Jordan, and Harold at pool at
Tashmoo Woods on Martha's Vineyard

Top photo: Harold Jara's family in Peru
Bottom photo: Grandson Koury and Patty McDowell with
their children: Deshaun, Kaidyn, Kyah, and Koury, Jr.

Top photo: Pendleton nieces Arnette, Abby Arlita and Addie and their children
Bottom photo left to right: Rachael with father Ronald
Walker and a friend at Rachael's cotillion

Top left photo: Olivia Walker on her prom night
Top right: George Pendleton with cousin Karen Walker
Bottom photo: cousin Wesley Harvey with his children -
Whitney, Wesley, Debbie, Wesley II, Summer and Grant

George and Garry Pendleton with lions in Italy, and aunts in Florida

Top photo: George at a neighbors birthday party in London, England
Bottom photo: Garry, at the same birthday party

Top photo: Daughter-in-law Shandolyn McDowell with dad Al at wedding
Bottom photo: Richard and Shandolyn Crouse dancing at their wedding

Top photo: Henry and Claudette with friends at wedding
At table Gretchen Underwood, Lynette and Bob Glover, Liz Walker
Standing from right to left: Tom Farrington, Joyce Williams,
Juarez Farrington, Harry Graham, Claudette, Henry, Rommie,
Winston English and Shan's niece and nephew
Bottom photo: Linda Crouse and dad Henry

236

Top photo: Julia with her mom Jo-Ann, and dad Brahim
Bottom photo: Candy Metcalf and Alane Ciriello

Top photo: Hillary Bridges with mom Renee and sister Lauren
Bottom photo: cousin Ronald Walker at his swearing-in as Secretary
of Labor and Workforce Development for Massachusetts

Top photo: Regan Wilmarth Benson and Janine Carr
Bottom photo: Morgan, Kaye and McCall Allen

Top photo: McCall Allen
Middle photo: Tasha and Mark Williams
Bottom photo: Tomeeka Farrington Mill

Top photo: Nix and Sarah Walker
Bottom photo: Victor and Regan Benson with older
son Tristan and younger son Cayden

Top photo: Robyn Glover
Bottom photo: Andrea and Janine Carr

Top photo: Shawnda and Ronald Walker with Governor
Deval Patrick officiating at their wedding
Bottom photo: Walkers entering wedding reception after the ceremony

Top photo: The Walker's Wedding Photo
Bottom photo: Lynette and Skip Griffin

Top photo: Skip and Lynette's wedding ceremony with Liz Walker officiating
Bottom photo: Andre Traylor, brother, George and
father George at Andre's wedding

Top photo: Crouse wedding
Bottom photo: Henry Crouse, with Claudette as he is
the "Guest of Honor "at Galway, Ireland's 500
Birthday Celebration

Ken Olsen President of Digital Equipment Corporation with Henry Crouse

*Top photo: Claudette with girlfriends at her Christmas party:
right to left- Claudette Crouse, Michele Carr, EJ Jones, Anne
Ashmore-Hudson, Sylvia Carr, Marva Gibson, Bea Curry
Bottom photo: Marva, Bea, Anne, and Claudette*

Top photo right to left: Donna Levy Wray, Vivian Beard, Claudette,
Betty Francis, Marion Grayer, Anne Ashmore-Hudson. Michele Carr
Middle photo right to left: Betty Francis, Claudette,
Vivian Beard, and Donna Levy Wray
Bottom photo left to right: Vivian, Vivian Pinn, Louise Johnson,
Claudette, Anne Ashmore-Hudson, and Marion Grayer

Top left: Donna Levy Wray, Henry and Juarez Farrington,
Top right photo: Dottie and Gerold McLeod
Bottom photo left: Bea Curry
Bottom right photo: Claudette on way to her Links installation

Top photo left to right: JudyAnn Bigby, Beverly Edgehill and Susan Bannister
Bottom photo: Donna Wilmarth and Paul Cefola

Top photo left to right: Darryl Settles, Gordon Bannister and Jeff Otten
Bottom photo left to right: Daya Fields and Lovita Johnson

Top photo: Joyce Williams
Bottom photo: Kathy Long Thurman

Top photo: Colette Phillips
Bottom photo: Rob Williams

Linda Whitlock

Vivian Pinn and Henry Wiggings in Kenya

*Page of cousin Howard and Fannie Dunaway with son
Mark and Claudette visiting Tampa Florida*

Top photo left to right: Jacqui and Wayne Budd and Marion Grayer
Bottom photo left to right: James Barnes, Dani Monroe,
Doug Wilder and Claudette and Henry Crouse

Top photo left to right: Juarez Farrington, Jackie Benson Jones, Betty Francis and Julia Monroe at Betty's going away luncheon
Middle photo left to right: James "Tally" Huson and Henry Crouse in Croatia
Bottom photo: Jeff and Ardell Otten

Top photo: Jeff Otten at Martha's Vineyard ferry
Middle: photo Henry Crouse and Jeff Otten
Bottom photo: Ed Fredkin and Jeff Otten on boat in Bermuda

Top photo: Jeff Otten talking with Gus White
Bottom photo: Jeff Otten, Henry Crouse and Ron Homer at a Crouse party

Top photo: Leon and Sherry Wilson at a party on Martha's Vineyard
Bottom photo: Lisa Owens and Darryl Settles in Crouse photo room

Top photo: Claudette, with John and Candi Jenkins celebrating the holidays
Bottom photo left to right: Sylvia Carr and Renee Bridges on the Vineyard

Top photo left to right: Claudette, Wanda Hinton, Betty Francis and Sylvia
Carr at James and Anne Ashmore-Hudson's wedding in Charlestown, S. C.
Middle photo left to right: Duane Jackson, Sylvia Carr and Debbie
Jackson at Bernie and Carol Fulps wedding in St. Thomas
Bottom photo back row left to right: Ronnie Lytle, Adrienne
Williams, Claudette, Gretchen Underwood, a friend, Diedre
Russell, bottom row, left to right, Valerie Jackson, Cheryl Homer
and Lynette Glover at Crouse party on Martha's Vineyard

Top photo left to right: Paul Johnson, Roger Matthews, Claudette,
Richard Carr and Bud Moseley at Crouse holiday party
Bottom photo left to right: Kathy Taylor and
Karen Sykes at a nonprofit fundraiser

Top photo left to right: Maynard Jackson, Henry Crouse,
Russell Jackson, Bill Lytle and Ron Homer
Middle photo left to right: Michele Carr, Gloria and
Marshall Clarke, Ron Homer and Anne Ashmore-Hudson -
Left photo: Loretta O'Brien and aunt Seal Medley
Bottom photo: John, Liz Walker and Claudette at Crouse House Warming

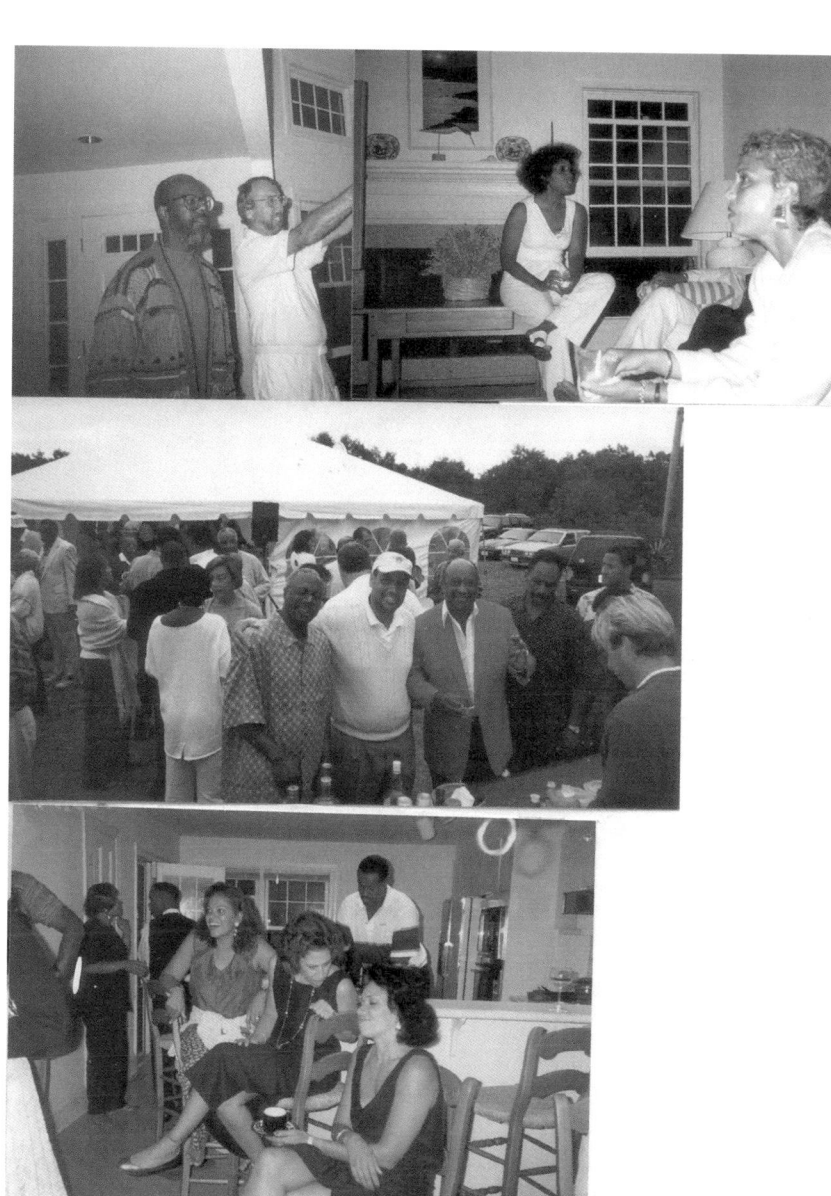

Top photo left to right: Debbie Jackson, Louise Johnson,
Bennie Wiley and a friend at the Fulp's wedding
Middle photo left to right: Fran Bernat, Kathy Taylor, Sylvia Carr
and Dorothy Terrell at Bible Study Retreat on the Vineyard
Bottom photo left to right: Donna Wilmarth, Bashie Young, Kathy
Taylor, Carol Fulp and Louise Johnson at Vineyard party
Bottom right photo: Guys on the Vineyard: sitting Russell Jackson,
Obie, Henry, standing right to left, Harris Gibson, Richard Taylor, John
Christian, Bill Lytle, Paul Jonhson, David VanAllen, and Bob Glover

Ladies at the BachMar Christmas party,
Sitting, left to right: Louise Johnson, Carolyn Hebsgaard, Paula Wright -
Standing left to right: Marion, Claudette, Michele, Kimmie, Ayanna and Fran
Bottom photo: Friends in Bermuda- left to right Ed Fredkin, Joyce
Fredkin, Michele Carr, Ardell Otten, Claudette, Henry, and Jeff Otten

Top photo left to right: EJ Jones, Janet Morris and Claudette
Middle photo: Vernon and Furman Jones
Bottom photo: Betty Francis and Furman Jones

Top photo left to right: Gordon Bannister, Claudette, Henry
and Sue Bannister celebrating Thanksgiving
Bottom photo: Karen Lieff with Frank at the Boston Ballet Gala

Top photo left to right: Karen, Jim, and Pat Long
Middle photo left to right: Kathy Epps, her friend, and Michele Carr
Bottom photo left to right: Kim Budd, Kimmie Jackson and
Becky McLeod at Claudette's Christmas meeting

Top photo sitting: Richard and Michele Carr and Claudette and Henry Crouse
Standing: Cheryl and Ron Homer and Fran Bernat
Bottom photo left to right: Fran, Anne, Claudette and
Louise at Crouse 10th Wedding Anniversary

273

*Top photo left to right: Claudette, Ronnie, Anne and Michele at Fulp wedding
Bottom photo left to right: Brenda Braithwaite, Dennis Tourse, Anne and
James Hudson, Carol Fulp and Robbie Tourse at Anne's going away party*

Top photo: Carmen Fields with daughter Karly and husband Lorenz Finison
Bottom photo left to right: Carol Benson, Donna
Wilmarth and Regan Wilmarth Benson

*Top photo Friends at a fundraiser left to right: Anne and Duffy Covington,
on stairs Dani Monroe, Liz Walker, Harry Graham and Henry Crouse
Bottom photo at table right to left: Helen. Claudette and
Robbie, standing, Anne and Donna, celebrating girls getaway
at Anne Ashmore-Hudson's home in Seabrook, S.C.*

Top photo left to right: Bill Coleman, Flash Wiley,
Tom Farrington and David Fields
Middle photo left to right: Deborah Bernat and Donna Wilmarth
Bottom photo left to right: Cliff and Marion Grayer and Richard Taylor

Top photo front, left to right: Claudette, Kathy, Cheryl, Marion, Michele,
Carolyn, Juarez and Cheryl, celebrating Guardsmen Weekend
Middle photo left to right: Pat Long, Bea Curry and Donna Levy Wray
Bottom photo left to right: Nancy Jordan, Claudette and Cindy Carter

Top photo front row, left to right: Claudette, Cheryl, Brian and Ron Homer, back row- Kathy and "T." Thompson and Henry Crouse Bottom photo sitting, left to right: Winston English, Gretchen Underwood, Bill and Joan Reals, standing, Harry Graham, Liz Walker, Claudette and Henry Crouse

Top photo left to right: Michael LeBlanc, Betty Francis, Carolyn
Coverdale, Betty Francis and Claudette at Betty's going away party
Middle photo left to right: Betty Francis and Marva Gibson
Bottom photo left to right: Betty, Claudette and Anne in
front of Henry's plane on Martha's Vineyard

Top photo left to right: Cindy Carter, Kathy Taylor, Marion and Cliff Grayer and Claudette having fun on Martha's Vineyard
Middle photo left to right: Carol Kelly, Diedre Russell, Kathy Taylor, Claudette Crouse, with guys on the Vineyard
Bottom photo left to right: Bennie Wiley, Claudette, Claudette and Bill Lytle

Top photo left to right: Designer Rommie, George Pendleton
Alane Ciriello, Henry, Shan and Richard Crouse
Bottom photo left to right: Claudette, David Fields,
Garry Pendleton and Richard Crouse

Top photo: Alane and George on St. Martin
Bottom photo: Victor and Regan Benson at Globoforce conference

Top photo left to right: David Fields, Marian Taylor, Claudette and Henry, Larry Whiteside, Cliff Grayer, and Russ McCabe
Bottom photo: Marion Grayer and Wanda Hinton

*Barbara Morgan, Henry and Tom Farrington on
Jeff and Ardell's Vineyard patio*

285

Top photo left to right: Myrna Cohn, Claudette and Ermajeanne Jones
Bottom photo: Duffy and Ann Covington

Top photo left to right: Priscilla Douglas, Gail Jackson, Claudette and a friend
Bottom photo left to right: Ray Hammond, Claudette and
Richard Rien at the Topf Center for Dance Education

Top photo: *Claudette and Richard Crouse at the Boston Ballet Gala*
Bottom photo: *Claudette Crouse and Shawnda Walker at a meeting*

*Top photo left to right: Claudette, Anne, Rita Scott,
and James Hudson at a villa in Croatia
Bottom photo: Claudette in the red dress
at her bosses party in London, England*

Top photo left to right: Henry with Ken Olsen and General George Doriot, and others on Digital tour on plants in Germany
Bottom photo left to right: Soon to be President Barak Obama, Claudette Crouse, Dorothy Terrell, and Al Brown at Martha's Vineyard fundraiser

Top photo left to right: Harold Epps, Richard Carr and a friend
Bottom photo: Harold and Jordan Jara

Left to right: Claudette Crouse, Kimmie Jackson and
Carolyn Hebsgaard in Buenos Aries, Argentina

Top photo left to right: Claudette Crouse, Marion Grayer, Bennie
Wiley and Elaine Whiteside at a Crouse Carlisle, MA party
Bottom photo left to right: Nancy and Arthur Altman
and Claudette Crouse at a fundraiser

Top photo left to right: Henry, Claudette, Sue, Gordon, Juarez and
Sue's parents, Frank and Ruth Richards at Thanksgiving dinner
Bottom photo in front row: Dora Lewin and Henry Crouse, seated
in next row is Joyce Fredkin at Joel and Dana Otten's wedding

294

*Top photo left to right: Sabrina Williams, Paula Wright, Michele
Carr and Carolyn Hebsgaard at Claudette Christmas dinner
Middle photo left to right: LA friends hosting Claudette and Henry
on their way to the Far East, including Diedre and Russell Jackson,
Larkin and Cynthia Arnold, and Charles Anne Johnson
Bottom photo left to right: Maynard Jackson, Henry Crouse,
Russell Jackson, Bill Lytle, and Ron Homer*

Top photo left to right: Juarez Farrington, Claudette,
Susan Bannister and her mother Ruth Richards
Bottom photo: Julia Pendleton with grandmother
Claudette Crouse at a Beyoncé concert

Top photo left to right: Rachael Walker, Karen Walker
and Karen's mother, Lorena Hodges
Middle photo left to right: Olivia Walker and Hodges family at dinner
Bottom photo left to right: Karen Hodges Walker, Claudette
Hodges Pendleton Crouse, and Lorena Hodges
Right photo: Lorena, Karen and Claudette

*Top photo left to right: Henry and Claudette
Crouse with Henry Wiggins in Kenya
Bottom photo left to right: Donna Levy Wray, Vivian
Beard, Claudette and Betty Francis*

Top photo: Eddy Benoit and Andre Traylor
Bottom photo: Eugenia and Bernie Bickerstaff at
Crouse party on Martha's Vineyard

Top photo left to right: Bernie Fulp and Darryl Settles
Bottom photo: Sylvia and M.L. Carr

Top photo Left to right sitting: Paula Vandever, Ardell Otten, Clemmie Cash, Diane Suda, Leslie George, standing right to left: Sandra King, Jackie Hawkinson, Loretta Sherblom, Joan Reals, and Mary Jo Meisner The Dividend Investment Club on a retreat on Martha's Vineyard Bottom photo left to right: Claudette Crouse, Valerie Wilder, and Margie Topf at The Boston Ballet gala

Top photo: Henry Crouse at Claudette's graduation party
Middle left photo: Claudette, David, Karen and
Howard celebrating Claudette's graduation
Far right photo: Arthur and Nancy Altman, with Henry
and Zerky at the Altman's summer home
Bottom photo left to right: Sylvia Carr, Cheryl Matthews,
Lynette Glover, Anne Ashmore-Hudson, Louise Johnson, Liz
Walker, France's Moseley, and Juarez Farrington
Sitting: Claudette Crouse and Cheryl Homer at a luncheon honoring Liz Walker

Top photo left to right: Fran, Anita White, Michele, Claudette and Donna
Middle photo: Claudette at her 50th birthday party
Bottom photo: We are in Washington, D.C. for Sharon Pratt
Kelly's inauguration as Mayor of The District of Columbia

*Top photo left to right: Arrik Crouse and Claudette
and Henry Crouse in St. Moritz
Middle photo: Garry, Jo-Ann with Jordan Jara
Bottom photo: Alane and George at Crouse Christmas breakfast*

Top photo: Friends at Sylvia Carr's surprise birthday party
Bottom photo: Claudette, Anita White and Ronnie Lytle

Top photo left to right: Clemmie Cash, Anne, and Donna Wilmarth
Middle photo: Sylvia Carr singing at her party
Bottom photo left to right: Janine Carr, Michele Carr, Anne, Fran
Jordan and Michael Carr: All waiting to surprise Sylvia

Top photo left to right: Sylvia, Juarez Farrington, Sylvia and Andrea Carr
Bottom photo left to right: Donna and Michele dancing at Sylvia's party

Top photo left to right: Ronnie and Marva having a
drink at Crouse party on the Vineyard
Middle photo: Delete it is a duplicate
Bottom photo left to right: Bill Lytle, Gretchen Underwood
and a friend at Crouse Vineyard party

Top photo left to right: Ronnie Lytle, Claudette Crouse, Cheryl Homer, and Ronnie at a Crouse Vineyard party
Bottom photo left to right: Bill Lytle and Ron Homer

Top photo left to right: Claudette, Gretchen Underwood, Valerie
Jackson and Henry having fun on Martha's Vineyard
Middle photo left to right: Cliff and Marion Grayer, Henry and Claudette Crouse
Bottom photo on left: Anne Ashmore-Hudson, across
table, Rita Scott and Henry Crouse in Croatia

*Top photo left to right: Ardell Otten, Donna Wilmarth and
Claudette Crouse on a friends porch on Martha's Vineyard
Bottom photo: Alane Ciriello and Kevin Anelli at Crouse anniversary celebration*

311

Top photo: The Party Committee for Betty Francis' going away party - left to right: Michele Carr, Anne Ashmore-Hudson, Marion Grayer, Betty Francis, Claudette Crouse, Vivian Beard and Donna Levy Wray
Middle photo left to right: Donna, Vivian, Claudette and Betty
Bottom photo left to right: Family Friend Vivian, Vivian Pinn, Louise Johnson Claudette Crouse, Anne Ashmore-Hudson, and Marion Grayer, celebrating Claudette's birthday

Top photo left to right: Debbie Jackson, Lynette Glover, Liz Walker,
Kathy Taylor, Claudette, Gloria White Hammond, and Fran Bernat
Middle photo of The Entire Bible Study Group - Front row: Kathy,
Debbie, Claudette, Rena, Sylvia and Fran - right to left, second row,
Gail Lenora, Carol, Jackie, Liz, Gloria, Dorothy and Lynette
Bottom photo: Henry and Claudette at the Palace Hotel in St. Moritz Switzerland

Claudette's Dividend Sisters

Bottom let up: Diane Ripstein and Sandra King; Claudette Crouse; Diane Ripstein, Leslie George, Diane Suda, Patricia OConnor, and Jackie Hawkington; Top left: Claudette Crouse, Nan Niland, Diane Ripstein and Amy Etherington; Top middle left: Diane Suda, Nancy Hsiung, Amy Etherington, Nan Hsuing and Diane Suda; Left Middle second row: left to right: Linda Whitlock, Sandra King, CarmenFields, and Nancy Hsuing; Priscilla, Claudette, and Nan, far right, middle row: Claudette Far Right bottom row: Maryjo Meisner; Bottom row, middle right: Maryjo, Amy, Wendy, and Nancy Bottom row, middle left: Marita Rivero, Claudette, Sandra, and Loretta

Left to right: Claudette Crouse; Diane Suda, Nan Niland;
Marian Heard; Loretta Sherbloom; Colette Phillips, Amy
Etherington; Sandra King; and MaryJo Meisner

Left to right: Loretta Sherblom; Carmen Fields; MaryJo Meisner;
Priscilla Douglas; Wendy Warring; Amy Etherington; Claudette
Crouse; Diane Ripstein; Diane Suda; Nancy Hsuing; Patricia
OConnor; Sandra King, Linda Whitlock; Nan Niland

M.L. and Sylvia Carr

Left to right: Henry and Claudette on a cruise and Alane Ciriello

Claudette Crouse walking forward

About the Author

CLAUDETTE CROUSE IS THE founder of The Crouse Women's Initiative—an organization dedicated to empowering women and girls to be their professional and personal best through training, mentoring and coaching. She is the former President and CEO of Topf Center for Dance Education, an organization providing inner-city youth the opportunity to reach their social and academic potential through the discipline and artistry of dance.

Originally from Philadelphia, PA, Claudette holds a Bachelor of Science degree in Psychology from the University of Massachusetts, and a Masters of Education degree in Consulting Psychology from Harvard University. She completed postgraduate training in Organization Development at the University of Michigan.

Claudette has over 25 years of innovative and successful professional business experience, both domestic and international. She has lived and worked in England, Switzerland, Holland, and Alaska. During her years at Digital Equipment Corporation, she successfully fulfilled a number of leadership roles. She effectively led a project team composed of executives from 10 European countries to found a Logistics Training Center in Holland.

She volunteers time to fund-raise for non-profits and community-based initiatives that enhance the lives of women and children. In the past, she worked with former WBZ-TV personality, Liz Walker, and the activist, Reverend Gloria Hammond, on fundraising efforts for "My Sister's Keeper," a human rights initiative to support women in Southern Sudan.

Claudette is also very much an activist. Among her many professional and volunteer activities, she has worked on several presidential and gubernatorial campaigns, including those of President Barrack Obama and Massachusetts Governor Deval Patrick's. She has served on the board of directors for many non-profit organizations in the Boston area.

When the Closed Heart Opens: Lessons Learned on the Journey of Life is Claudette's first book.

Claudette and her husband, Henry Crouse, a venture capitalist, live in Carlisle, MA.